Going Public

HOW TO MAKE YOUR
INITIAL
STOCK
OFFERING
SUCCESSFUL

Going Public

HOW TO MAKE YOUR
INITIAL
STOCK
OFFERING
SUCCESSFUL

Martin Weiss

LIBERTY HALL
PRESS™

LIBERTY HALL PRESS books are published by LIBERTY HALL PRESS, an imprint of TAB BOOKS. Its trademark, consisting of the words "LIBERTY HALL PRESS" and the portrayal of Benjamin Franklin, is registered in the United States Patent and Trademark Office.

FIRST EDITION
SECOND PRINTING

©1988 by Martin Weiss
Printed in the United States of America

Library of Congress Cataloging-in-Publication Data

Weiss, Martin.
   Going public / by Martin Weiss.
     p.   cm.
   Includes Index.
ISBN 0-8306-3012-0   ISBN 0-8306-7012-2 (pbk.)
   1. Going public (Securities)—United States. 2. Going public (Securities)—Law and legislation—United States. I. Title.
HG4963.W45 1987   90-6316
658.15'224—dc20   CIP

Contents

Introduction

THE PROCESS OF "GOING PUBLIC" IS COMPLICATED AND EXPENSIVE. Qualified professionals—accountants, attorneys, underwriters, consultants—are available, at a price, to help take you successfully through that program. These professionals know the laws, the rules, the procedures, and the tricks of their trades.

The initial public offering of a company is, however, an unusual business and emotional experience for most owners, executives and employees alike, and they will be called upon to make crucial decisions in new and unfamiliar areas. As with any business activity, the better prepared you and your staff are and the more you know about the process, the pressures, the problems and the dangers, the greater your chances will be for short-term and long-term success.

A number of guides have been prepared to aid the owner or CEO of a growing company considering "going public." Most of those publications are prepared by or under the auspices of a CPA firm, a law firm, or an investment banking firm. While the formal advice given in those guides is technically accurate and correct, they have been written from a totally different perspective from that faced by you, the businessman/owner.

This book addresses, in a very different manner, the problems you may encounter and the questions you will have. My comments, suggestions, and concerns are presented as if I were by your side—and on your side. I have tried to minimize the technical content and maximize the practical value in the subjects covered. This book is not a substitute for professional legal or accounting advice. It will, however, be of considerable value to you in achieving a successful public offering in the most inexpensive, efficient, and satisfactory manner possible.

1

Deciding to Go Public

MANY BUSINESS OWNERS VIEW THE POSSIBILITY OF AN *INITIAL PUBlic offering* (IPO) of their company's stock as the ultimate dream—the fulfillment of years of hard work, expressed in terms of wealth, prestige, recognition, and power. To others, that dream represents a nightmare—something to be feared and avoided at all costs, even at the expense of restricting the growth and potential of their company. In reality, the successful public sale of a part of the equity of your company is neither a fantasy nor a nightmare, but rather the objective of a strategic business decision made after detailed consideration of all the pros and cons. Like most business decisions, the earlier you plan and more prepared you are, the better the results.

Things to Think About

One of the early considerations in making the decision to "go public" is the emotional preparedness (or lack thereof) of the owner(s) and the management team for the new role of running a public company. Managing a company having many, many shareholders with whom there is a special fiduciary responsibility will be very different from when there was only one owner or a few partners. Recognize and accept

1

that significant changes will probably be required in the existing decision-making processes, in disclosures of information (such as related-party transactions, officers' compensation and fringe benefits), in recordkeeping, and perhaps in the structure and composition of the management team, board of directors and other outside advisors. The previous success of the management team and methodology which built the business to the point where a public offering of its stock can be considered, is not necessarily an automatic indicator that they will be equally as successful under the various constraints and requirements of the "public company environment." Not every owner or management group seeking to take a company public deals with this basic question in an unbiased and objective manner.

Generally speaking, "going public" does not mean the loss of *control* of the company, even though that concern may be one of the first which goes through an owner's mind. For practical purposes, only a relatively small proportion of the stock ownership and/or voting authority needs to remain in the hands of the original founders/owners/managers for them to retain effective operating control of the company. Most initial and subsequent public offerings should result in a fairly wide distribution of stock into many hands, even if a large following of *institutional investors* (mutual funds, pension funds, etc.) ultimately develops for the stock. Usually, the unfriendly takeover is a worry for the larger public company, not the small or midsize company. The loss of effective control over the affairs of the small or midsize company is more likely to occur as a result of being overly extended or heavily indebted to banks than because the majority of its stock is publicly held.

Although a public stock offering may be conducted directly by your company, the vast majority of stock offerings are arranged through an *investment banking firm* (IBF). Essentially, the IBF functions as an *underwriter* by buying the stock from your company under certain terms and conditions, and reselling the securities to the investing public, institutional investors, or other securities dealers.

Form S-1 and Form S-18 Registrations

The *Securities and Exchange Commission* (SEC) has very explicit standards regarding the information which must be disclosed in the *registration statement* and *prospectus* filed for the typical IPO. The information required includes both financial and non-financial data, presented in an organized format. In a *Form S-1* registration there are requirements such as the need for a five-year summary of earnings, with the most recent three years being audited; audited balance sheets for the last two years, and other very extensive financial statement disclosures. A *Form S-18* "simplified" registration may be used for offerings of up to $7.5 million in a single year. This new type of registration requires only two years' audited income statements and one year's audited balance sheet. Other financial disclosure requirements are reduced, and the registration statement may be filed at a regional SEC office rather than at Washington. This may result in significant time savings.

You should obtain several copies of recent IPOs from your local stockbroker and review the type and nature of factual information, disclosures, and data that must be included. You will probably find that, as a privately-owned company, it was never necessary to tell anyone so much confidential information about your business operations, compensation, and background. Once you enter the public market and as long as you remain an officer, director, or principal stockholder, you will remain subject to many rules and regulations regarding disclosure of certain financial transactions and other matters vis-à-vis the company, and certain personal activities.

Advance Planning and Preparation

A relationship with a CPA firm should be established as early as possible in the formation and/or development of the company. While it is possible for an accounting firm to go back and retroactively audit a two- or three-year period, it may not be practical because the outside accounting firm might not have been present when prior years' inventories were counted and valued, and thus may not be able to render an unqualified opinion on the financial reports for such periods. The future potential for a public offering of the stock of a company some years hence is a compelling reason for the owner to have regular annual audits of the financial statements of his company as early in its existence as possible.

Once it has been decided to actively pursue the goal of a public stock sale, the owner(s), the management team, and several key business advisors (including accountants, attorneys and others), must formulate and execute a carefully thought-out plan for a successful initial sale and a well-supported after-market for the stock.

You should engage the services of a streetwise financial consultant as soon as possible. A consultant who has had solid experience in evaluating and negotiating public offerings on behalf of his client companies will be invaluable to you; he can give you an unbiased assessment of the various underwriting proposals you will be receiving. He will give you advice regarding the underwriter's compensation requests, act as a buffer between you and the underwriter, and assist in obtaining the best possible deal for you. His fee should be repaid to you many times over through the savings he can generate by making sure you have the best underwriting arrangement possible. You cannot depend upon the IBFs with whom you are negotiating to protect your interests.

For a successful IPO, it is important for the company to "have a good story." Its outlook should appear bright and encouraging either because of its existing products and markets, or because of products, technology, and markets under development. This favorable outlook is translated into an expectation of increasing earnings and a higher stock price. While the historical record of the company and management are very important, the potential investor's anticipations for the future of the company will ultimately determine whether he buys the stock.

While the primary responsibility for selling your company's initial stock offering to the public will theoretically rest with the underwriter and their marketing *syndicate*, the company should start its own public and financial relations programs a year or so in advance of the target offering date. When you initially reach tentative agreement with an underwriter to undertake an offering, the *"quiet period"* starts. This period lasts from the date of the first decision to proceed with an offering until 90 days after the *effective date* of the offering. During this period, any publicity regarding the company can raise a serious legal question as to whether it is part of the stock-selling effort, that is, a pre-effective offering. Legally, the offering and selling effort can only be made by the prospectus. While the SEC has no objection to the regular and normal advertising done by a business, it is concerned about non-routine advertising, sales projections, forecasts and the like—anything which gives the appearance of trying to "hype" the interest in your offering. During the entire period, all advertising, public announcements, press releases, etc., from the company, its directors, officers, or executives, should first be cleared with your attorneys and those of the underwriter.

The price at which the company's stock will be sold in the initial offering is, in part, dictated by such factors as the type of industry it is in, how it is viewed vis-à-vis its competitors, the reputation and quality of its management, and its future prospects. Many of those factors are perceptions by the public, and thus can be shaped, molded, and influenced by the company. Engaging the services of a financial/public relations consultant may prove to be of immense value in constructing the desired image. You want your company (and later-on its stock) to be well-known and considered a desirable investment by the people and organizations that buy stock and by those who influence the investment decisions. An early start will enable the company to legally stimulate investor interest well in advance of the actual offering and help the owner and the company obtain the maximum per-share price at the initial offering and support it for some period beyond.

Build the image and stimulate the interest before the search for an underwriter begins. There is every probability that the image-building campaign will bring the IBFs knocking on your door to see if your company would be interested in a public offering of its stock.

The actual process of selecting an underwriter, preparing and filing a registration statement with the SEC, selling the stock, and receiving the proceeds normally takes about six months, but the internal planning, preparation, and orchestration for an IPO should be done by the company's owners, management and advisors at least one or two years in advance.

2

Why and When
Should You Go Public?

THE ANSWERS TO THE QUESTIONS "WHY SHOULD YOU GO PUBLIC?" and "When should you go public?" are related and depend upon the interplay of a number of circumstances, some of which you can prioritize and manage, and others which you cannot control at all.

Why Go Public?

The three most common reasons for taking a privately owned company public through an IPO are:

- to raise money for working capital, repayment of debt, expansion of plant and equipment, etc.,

- to increase the net worth, enabling the company to expand its borrowing capacity or obtain more favorable credit terms and conditions, and

- to allow the original owner(s) to convert equity in the company to cash by selling some of their stock in connection with the company's initial offering and/or creating a publicly traded stock which can be borrowed against or sold at some future time.

Each of the above reasons is predictable and within the power of the owner of a well-run business to anticipate and plan. If there is any possibility that going public may be in the future for your company, then you and the company must be prepared to act. That much is in your control, and you can't blame anyone else for failing to be ready when the opportunity and circumstances permit.

When to Go Public

As a businessman, you must be pragmatic and learn from what history and the experience of others have proven to be true, time and time again. While occasionally there may be exceptions, these factors generally represent reality:

- Money/capital is usually more available to you when you don't need it. Conversely, the most difficult and expensive time to raise capital or borrow money is often when you need it the most.

- No one can accurately predict the future of the stock market or the investment community, the price valuations they will place on businesses, or even their willingness to invest in any new stock offerings.

- A public offering takes time to accomplish, and even more time to plan and prepare. If you haven't been actively and properly getting ready for it, then you can expect the process to take at least a year.

- You will spend many thousands of dollars (perhaps as much as $300,000 in legal, accounting, printing, and other expenses) preparing the stock offering, with no guarantee that the offering will actually take place, or if it does, that you will get your target per-share price and raise all the capital you seek.

Going public is neither a rash, spur-of-the-moment decision nor something that can be repeatedly delayed—if you ever want to get it done successfully. There are periodic windows of opportunity when the stock market is receptive to your company, when your company is (or can be made) ready for the market, and when IPOs are more highly valued, more favorably received and easier to market. It is at those times that you must try to take advantage of the situation if at all possible, *even if your company does not need the money immediately*. Because you cannot predict the future, you cannot determine the perfect time to act, but you can, if ready, react at a good time and minimize the risk.

Years ago, a well-seasoned official of a prominent IBF, and a Wall Street veteran, gave some good financial advice to a group of business owners. He said, "When cookies are being passed around the dinner table, make sure you take your share of the cookies then, because you don't know if or when the plate will come around again." When Wall Street seems willing and able to give your company a sizeable amount of money at a fair price, think hard before you pass up that opportunity. You don't know when you will get the chance again.

You should also not permit your company's finances (or yours), to get into the situation where a quickly conceived public stock offering is the only viable alternative for the continued success or fiscal survival of the company. There are many examples of companies who utilized an excessive amount of short-term, demand debt to fund permanent growth or other activities which more properly should have been supported by an expansion of net worth. When they had to go public, they found that the capital market cycle was unfavorable for IPOs. In the end, they either were unable to raise the needed equity capital, or else they had to accept a significantly deflated value for the shares sold.

Remember too that the company will have spent a considerable amount of money preparing the registration statement and, when the registration statement and documents are complete and accepted by the SEC, the underwriter may call you with bad news. For example, he might say:

- "The market is acting very weak."
- "The syndicate is having trouble marketing the issue."
- "We think you will have to drop the issue price to sell it."
- "We think you will have to shrink the size of the deal and reduce the number of shares offered."

You may find yourself in a difficult situation. Are you able to postpone the issue and wait out the market (or the underwriter's pressure) for a while? Have you retained a reasonable amount of financial flexibility because you have not let fiscal pressures force you into an inopportune public offering timetable?

The key point to recognize is the need for you and your company to be as much in control of the situation as possible—to have options available to you if events don't work out as planned. This can only be achieved by pre-planning, by picking and choosing the times to act or not act, and by having alternative courses of action.

3

Early Considerations

UNDER IDEAL CIRCUMSTANCES, THE INTERNAL PLANS TO GO PUBLIC should be developed and implemented one or two years in advance so that the owners and the company are not only prepared emotionally but also organizationally (competent staff, no more one-man show) and structurally (adequate records and management information systems).

How Good Is Your Staff?

In light of the special expertise required to meet the complex registration and reporting requirements of the SEC, part of the companywide preparation process is the need for the owners to objectively assess the prior experience, talent, and qualifications of the company's chief financial officer, corporate attorneys, and CPA firm.

In many businesses, it is typical that the senior accounting person (whatever the title) has done quite well in handling the routine, day-to-day accounting responsibilities, but might not have been participating in, or recognized as an important part of, management. In the public company environment, an articulate, versatile, and knowledgeable chief financial officer is an absolute necessity. The chief financial officer and the staff he manages have to be capable of promptly and accurately providing the special reports, information, and data required of a public company. There will be many situations where he will be an active spokesman, key negotiator, and top-level representative for the company, often on his own. The overall scope and impact of the position will expand considerably. Do you have confidence in his ability to fulfill these new technical and personal job requirements? Are the other top members of your management team prepared to treat him as a peer? An honest assessment of the situation may result in the need to recruit a more capable individual for the top financial position in your company, and it should be done as early in the process as possible.

To avoid loss of time, unnecessary expense, and potential legal liability for false or misleading information, it is vital that the legal and accounting work for the IPO be performed by persons well versed in SEC practices. Irrespective of how well the relationships with your outside attorneys and accountants have been working in the past, you might find that new or additional professional help is now needed. Both firms will be eager to earn larger fees from your company in connection with the offering and in the future, so they cannot be totally objective on this question. Obviously, you want to respect their past efforts, support, and loyalty, but you must be as realistic as possible.

It is not unusual for the growing company to replace its accountants and/or attorneys when its needs exceed the capabilities, experience, and resources of the current firms. It is also possible that the underwriter might request that you use a larger, more prestigious accounting and/or law firm in connection with the underwriting. Discuss this matter frankly and openly with your current firms and with other knowledgeable individuals whose opinion in such matters you would respect.

Will Your Records Pass the Test?

Assuming that the company has been in business for some time, there exists an "official" financial- and business-performance track record. The typical company has issued financial statements, established inventory values, filed tax returns, made loans to officers, and entered into a few contracts or leases with insiders. In general, it has conducted itself as a normal, privately-owned corporation by conserving its financial resources, maximizing the owner's net income and not attracting too much attention.

More than likely then, the historical record might not quite portray the company's past performance in the way it will need to be portrayed for the IPO. Some of the legitimate accounting methods or tax treatment alternatives previously employed might reflect an opposite picture of what you would like to show in order to obtain the best price for the stock at the IPO. By starting a couple of years in advance, you have the opportunity to review your tax and accounting practices with the accounting firm and make changes at a pace that is appropriate for the circumstances. The possible impact of those changes on the company's cash flow, taxable income, and balance sheet during the transition period must be taken into consideration.

Now that the company will come under public scrutiny, attorneys will also undertake a detailed review of all its existing legal arrangements, including the corporate structure, charter, bylaws, contracts, leases, loan documents, insider agreements, trademarks, patents, licenses, lawsuits, and any other area of potential legal liability. Renegotiations, adjustments, and changes might be necessary to bring things into an acceptable condition.

The legal files of a suprisingly large number of otherwise well-run and well-organized private firms are totally unprepared for such a review. While you and your regular attorneys might have treated this subject casually in the past, a complete housecleaning, updating, and review are vital before outside attorneys are brought in to prepare the documents for the offering. Typically, the minutes of the board of directors meetings are incomplete or non-existent. The company might not be officially registered to do business in all the states in which it conducts its business, or the corporate charter and bylaws might need amendment. These and numerous other details can seriously impact the costs of preparing for the offering, as well as the success of the offering itself. To correct these matters after the registration process has begun, with a number of very expensive outside attorneys and CPAs doing the work at your expense, can be an enormous burden. It is also possible that the nature and extent of corrections, revisions, and modifications might be so great that the registration will have to be postponed for quite some time.

You Can't Bluff Your Way

In your initial discussions with potential underwriters, and later on during the in-person presentations to members of the marketing syndicate and potential investors, you will have to explain such things as the company's mission and objectives, its existing strengths and weaknesses, and its reasons for raising additional capital. While name recognition and a well-constructed business image are powerful forces in achieving a successful offering, you cannot avoid having a sound business plan for the future of your company.

It might seem elementary to discuss the need for a sound business plan for the future, but in many organizations, the plan, if it exists, is locked inside the CEO's head and no other executive knows all of it or understands his part in it. You and the other members of the executive staff must be able to articulate common goals and objectives for the company—how the plan will be implemented, what resources are needed or available, and where the risks are. The plan should deal with short-, middle-, and long-range time frames. It should display a complete grasp of the problems and challenges to be faced internally and externally, and should have a reasonably good chance of being successful. An essential element of any good business plan is the existence of control procedures to guide progress from one objective to another, and benchmarks to help assess progress (or lack of progress). A business plan is never complete; it requires updating, revalidation, and review. Numerous books and consulting services are available to assist you and your management team in developing and writing a business plan.

Do not underestimate the ability of a quality IBF to have considerable in-depth knowledge of your industry and the problems and prospects of your company. You will not be able to bluff your way out of your lack of a good business plan.

4

Contacting an Underwriter

NOT EVERY COMPANY WILL ATTRACT THE ATTENTION OF AN IBF AND be ardently "wooed and pursued." More often than not, the company must take the first step in contacting the investment banking community regarding a public offering. This initial phase must be conducted in a professional and organized manner, whether done by the company's own personnel or an outside consultant.

The Outside Consultant

If an outside consultant is used by the company, he or she should have the complete confidence of the owners, directors and management. While certainly not infallible, the consultant, if properly selected, will have considerably more experience in such matters than members of the company's staff. If you hire a consultant, heed his or her advice. If you're not going to listen to a consultant, then don't hire one.

When selecting a consultant, several factors should be considered:

- Does the consultant have a successful track record with companies the size of yours, offerings in the aggregate dollar range sought by your company, or in businesses similar to yours? Some consultants have better contacts with less prominent IBFs, firms that would be more likely to underwrite the smaller offering. Some consultants are more closely associated with the IPOs of high-technology companies.

- How is the "chemistry" between the company team and the consultant? There must be mutual trust and understanding if the relationship is to achieve success. The consultant's ongoing relationship with "Wall Street" is more important to him or her than your particular deal. Neither party should place the other's reputation or credibility in jeopardy.

- Does what the consultant say sound too good to be true? If so, it probably is just that. No consultant can or should promise that he or she can get everything the company wants, when it is wanted, and on unrealistic terms. Wall Street is too fickle and the market too volatile for that kind of empty promise.

Check out the references of any consultant before you hire, and beware of the "name-dropper." When in doubt, trust your instincts.

Where Do You Find an IBF to Call?

Whether a consultant is used or not, the approach is fairly similar—a phone call to make initial contact and describe the who-what-when-and-why, followed up by a "package" of data on the company.

The consultant should know which firms to contact, but the company may not know where to begin if it is doing it alone. While the process can start as simply as your calling up IBFs listed in the local or Manhattan Yellow Pages and asking to speak to the senior vice president of the corporate finance department, some sort of pre-established personal introduction is infinitely better. The headquarters of most major IBFs are located in New York City, but many of the larger firms have local branch offices in major cities throughout the country. These offices often have an executive assigned to respond to local corporate financing inquiries and opportunities. Larger cities or metropolitan areas also have regional IBFs, firms that do not have national prominence but, within certain geographic limits, have an excellent reputation.

You might already have a personal contact with an IBF through an individual stock broker with whom you have been conducting your personal or company's investment activities. While probably not an expert in the firm's corporate finance and underwriting activities, the broker can usually arrange an introduction with appropriate individuals at the local office or at headquarters. There should be no initial or contingent fee for such an introduction. The broker will be compensated by the IBF if it ultimately does the underwriting. Often, one of the company's officers, directors, or corporate attorneys has a personal contact at an IBF that is worthwhile to pursue.

Because of his experience, a consultant might contact more than one IBF at the very beginning. If the company is doing without the services of a consultant, start out by contacting only one IBF. Before you rush out and contact several firms, you and other key members of your team should get some experience in what an IBF will typically ask, look for, and expect. By learning from the initial contact, you will be able to better prepare the information needed to present the company's story in the best light.

The Initial Conversation

Your first contact with the IBF will probably be conducted over the phone with a member of the firm's corporate finance department. To give the IBF an overview of your situation, you will be asked some questions regarding the amount of capital sought, your company's historical, current, and projected annual sales volume, its profit history, the nature of its products and markets, its market share, and a few other details.

For a number of perfectly valid reasons the IBF may immediately indicate no real interest in your company. The size of the offering may be too small or (rarely) too large for them. They may have a relationship with one of your competitors and, thus, a conflict of interest. Or they may feel that you and/or your firm have a reputation with which they do not wish to be associated. If they do not seem anxious to follow up on your contact, see if you can get them to suggest other firms that might be more appropriate for you, and get the names of individuals to contact at those firms. An IBF knows the interests, strengths, and weaknesses of other IBFs and might be able to save you a considerable amount of time in your search.

If your situation appears interesting to an IBF, they will ask that you send them a package of information on your company for their review. The contents, form, and structure of the information within this package is extremely important.

The Information Package

Make no mistake about it—the first information package you send to the IBF is an important selling document. While it is a sales tool, it must not, however, be misleading or the product of a vivid imagination. It should convey the image of a professionally managed, well-run organization with a sound business plan to meet the current and future challenges facing the company. While the package must be complete, it shouldn't be overwhelming in detail. Much of the material in the package is similar to the information that would ultimately be disclosed in a registration statement and prospectus filed with the SEC, but at this time it can be presented and worded in a much more upbeat and optimistic style.

The IBF will expect to see the following information presented in an organized fashion:

1. A brief synopsis of the company as it exists today—its name, what it makes, sells, or provides, and the market(s) it addresses. Indicate current annual sales and earnings.

2. How much money is being sought, why it is needed, and for what it is to be used. Indicate if any of the present shareholders want to sell some of their holdings in connection with the offering by the company. Note that the information regarding the amount and use of the proceeds must be supported by and be consistent with the business plan included elsewhere in the package. If the new capital will have an immediate, positive effect on earnings (e.g., the reduction of interest expense as a result of the repayment of debt), this should be pointed out.

3. A fairly detailed write-up of the "why and what" that sets your company apart from its peers. This may revolve around such factors as brand-name recognition, technological innovations, historical industry leadership, importance in market share or technology, or any other factors that set your company apart from and above the ordinary. Advantages of your products over those of your competitors should be pointed out, and done so in terms that a non-industry or a non-technical person can understand. Never assume that the reader will be familiar with the nuances and subtleties of your industry. The information that you provide must enable the reader to follow a clear and logical sequence from what your

company "has going for it" to future profitable growth. It may not, however, be enough to establish the "bona fides" of your company; you must also establish that the industry in which the company is engaged has significant growth potential. Use every opportunity to reference or quote from outside authoritative sources to support your claims. Industry trade or marketing associations, U.S. Government statistics, or other nationally recognized data banks make excellent sources to support both the historical information and future forecasts. Do not ignore the existence of your competitors, especially those that are well-known or have significant market share. Nothing will damage your credibility faster than to avoid any reference to competitors, because the IBF may be more cognizant of your competitors than of your company.

4. A digest of the business plan you intend to follow to meet the challenges and exploit the opportunities of the future. To address the future your plan must have an appreciation of present realities and a logical course of action, including resources needed. Product research and development should be discussed, as well as overall industry problems, trends, and directions. It is not necessary to disclose all your trade secrets or confidential plans at this point, but your presentation should be fairly complete.

5. Comparative and comprehensive profit and loss statements for at least five years (or since the company's inception, if less than five years old). Depending upon when the data is being supplied, interim profit and loss statements should be included. If the recent financial performance of the company, as reflected in the financial statements, shows some loss years or is otherwise unimpressive, include a frank explanation of how and why that happened and what action has been taken to avoid a recurrence. While the poor financial performance is a reflection on management, you cannot rewrite history. Your ability to analyze what went wrong and take corrective action is important.

6. Comparative balance sheets for the same period covered by the profit and loss statements.

7. Appropriate notes to the financial statements provided in #5 and #6 above, especially for the two most recent years.

8. Certified Public Accountant's opinion on at least the most recent annual financial statements, and an indication of how long the statements have been audited.

9. Product literature and catalog sheets describing the most important current and future products.

When you send the information package to the IBF, indicate that you will be contacting them in a few days to respond to any questions. Include an offer to meet with them, at their convenience, in the very near future to discuss matters in greater detail. Allow a reasonable time for them to study the data, but if you have not heard from them within five business days of their receipt of the package, call them. Time is not on your side; you want to know where they stand as soon as possible.

One or more members of the IBF's staff will read the information package and make an initial determination of their level of interest. Depending upon the authority level of your contact, the data may have to work its way up the chain of command until someone decides to either reject any further consideration or authorize more formal contact and discussions with you. Even if your first contact with the IBF was by personal visit, an information package will still be required.

If the response is negative, try to find out why. What were the factors that caused the IBF to reject consideration of your company? Listen carefully to their explanation and, if appropriate and valid, apply what you learn towards changing your approach, information, or tactics before contacting other IBFs.

The First Meeting

If the IBF's response indicates positive interest, a meeting is the next step. Usually, this meeting takes place at your company's headquarters or principal operating facility. The IBF usually sends down at least two individuals, one of whom is generally the closest thing to an expert on your industry or market that the IBF has available at that moment. You can never be exactly sure of how much of an expert he or she will really be, so don't draw any hasty conclusions and don't take things at face value. One of the company's owners or senior officers should be the chairman of the meeting. That person might also be the primary spokesperson for the company.

Allow a full day for the meeting, which should include a tour of the manufacturing and research departments, the showrooms and demonstration labs, the computer facilities, and any other impressive or significant areas. Make certain that the facilities are neat and well-maintained; first impressions do count. You should expect that the IBF's personnel will want to meet key members of the executive staff, including, as a minimum, the chief financial officer, the sales and/or marketing officer(s), and the engineering and/or research officer(s). The discussions that take place will touch on everything that was included in the information package, and then some. The tone will be informal, relaxed, and not as restricted as a formal presentation. Many impromptu and extemporaneous answers and statements will be given. Often, the IBFs personnel will carry on private conversations with some of the officers and subsequently compare their notes. The company executives, with whom the IBF will be talking, must not make remarks which refute or conflict with the data, information, or forecasts in the information package.

For the most part, the meeting will concentrate on matters relating to the company's business. But at some point the topic should get around to the details of the proposed public offering. At this stage of the discussions, do a lot more listening than talking. Ask questions, seek explanations, and don't assume anything.

When asked if you are having (or will have) discussions with other IBFs, say yes. Explain that the information package was sent to other IBFs, and you are awaiting responses. IBFs don't like you to talk to other firms, but it is in your best interest to do so. At the conclusion of the meeting, ask the IBF to give you an idea of their timetable, and when you might be hearing from them next. If they have requested additional data, send it to them as quickly as possible.

As soon as possible after the IBF's personnel leave, get your executives together to review and critique the meeting. Summarize your impressions, learn from your mistakes, and improve.

5

Key Factors
Influencing the Offering

THE AMOUNT OF MONEY WHICH CAN BE RAISED THROUGH A PUBLIC
offering and the offering price-per-share are affected by a combination
of several factors, including:

- the historical and future earnings capability of the company,
- the present stock market environment, as reflected in the
  price/earnings (P/E) ratio of similar companies already on the
  public market,
- the image of the company in the eyes of the investment
  community, especially regarding the company's potential for
  profitable growth,
- the percentage of additional stock ownership that the present
  owners are willing to allow in public hands,
- the amount of money the company wants to raise, and
- the impact of dilution.

To illustrate the impact of some of the various factors involved,
assume that a company has one million shares of common stock
authorized, of which 500,000 shares are in the hands of the present
owners and 500,000 shares are unissued. Suppose also, that the
company wants to raise approximately $5 million in additional capital,

and that none of the present owners intends to sell shares in connection with the public offering. Company earnings for the most recent fiscal year were reported at $840,000. Current earnings per share (EPS) are $1.68 ($840,000 total net earnings ÷ 500,000 shares outstanding).

The Price/Earnings Ratio

The P/E ratio for a publically traded stock is calculated by dividing the company's per-share market price by its current annual earnings per share. The P/E ratios for similar companies within the same industry may vary considerably, as can the average P/E ratios of different industries. P/E ratios are influenced by how the broad investment community feels about the general economic and investment climate. On a company and/or industry basis, the P/E ratio is influenced by the past and potential growth of that company or industry within the context of the present and anticipated economic climate.

If the average P/E ratio currently enjoyed by publicly held companies similar to yours is 12, then the approximate, aggregate market value for your company is equal to the total net earnings times the P/E ratio, or $840,000 × 12 = $10,080,000. At first glance, it may appear that the company could sell about 248,000 shares at $20.16 each ($1.68 EPS × 12 P/E) to raise the $5 million. But, if it sells that additional 248,000 shares, then an aggregate of 748,000 shares would be outstanding, with a resultant decrease in the EPS to $1.12 ($840,000 total net earnings ÷ 748,000 shares outstanding), and a reduction in the per-share market price to $13.44 at a P/E ratio of 12 ($1.12 EPS × 12 P/E). With an offering price of $13.44, it would take more than 372,000 shares to raise the $5 million target, which in turn triggers a further reduction of the potential per-share market price. This spiral is referred to as earnings *dilution*.

Effects of Earnings Dilution

Earnings dilution takes place when, all other things remaining equal, the worth of a share of stock decreases because the company has issued additional shares. Each share has a smaller piece of the company's earnings "pie" than it did before.

In the example above, approximately 500,000 additional shares must be sold at a per-share price of $10.08 to raise the $5 million if the P/E ratio is 12:

$$\text{EPS} = \frac{\$840{,}000 \text{ Total Earnings}}{500{,}000 \text{ Shares Outstanding} + 500{,}000 \text{ New Shares}} = \$0.84$$

Stock Price $=$ EPS $\times$ P/E Ratio $=$ $\$0.84 \times 12$ $=$ $\$10.08$ per share

Money Raised $=$ New Shares $\times$ Stock Price $=$ $500{,}000 \times \$10.08$
$=$ $\$5{,}040{,}000$

The earnings dilution in this example was 50%, since the per-share earnings were $1.68 before the new shares were issued and about $0.84 after.

The above calculations were based upon a P/E ratio of 12. If you examine the P/E ratios for the public companies similar to yours, you will probably find that each one has a different ratio and their range, for example, may be between a high of 20 and a low of 10. If you were able to get a P/E ratio of 20, significantly fewer new shares would have to be sold to raise the $5 million and there would be less dilution:

$$\text{EPS} = \frac{\$840{,}000 \text{ Total Earnings}}{500{,}000 \text{ Shares Outstanding} + 215{,}000 \text{ New Shares}} = \$1.17$$

Stock Price $=$ EPS $\times$ P/E Ratio $=$ $\$1.17 \times 20$ $=$ $\$23.40$ per share

Money Raised $=$ New Shares $\times$ Stock Price $=$ $215{,}000 \times \$23.40$
$=$ $\$5{,}031{,}000$

The earnings dilution in this example is only 30% because of the higher P/E ratio. In addition, a higher P/E ratio permits the original owners of the company's stock to retain a greater percentage of ownership than an offering done at a lower P/E ratio because fewer shares will have to be publically sold to raise the capital needed.

In the examples above, the costs of making the offering (legal and accounting fees, printing costs, underwriting discounts and commissions, etc.) were ignored. If the aggregate of such costs was to run approximately $800,000, in order for the company to net $5 million, the total offering would have to be for $5.8 million. With a P/E ratio of 20, approximately 265,000 shares must be sold at a price of $22.00 per share for the company to net $5 million:

$$\text{EPS} = \frac{\$840{,}000 \text{ Total Earnings}}{500{,}000 \text{ Shares Outstanding} + 265{,}000 \text{ New Shares}} = \$1.10$$

Stock Price = EPS × P/E Ratio = $1.10 × 20 = $22.00 per share

Money Raised = New Shares × Stock Price = 265,000 × $22.00
= $5,830,000

Proceeds to Company = Money Raised − Costs of Offering
= $5,830,000 − $800,000
= $5,030,000

The P/E ratio used in arriving at the offering price for your stock is, within limits, largely a matter of negotiation between you and the underwriter. The more favorable the image of your company and its prospects and potential, the better the chance to negotiate a P/E ratio at or above those enjoyed by your peer companies already in the market. If the recent performance history of the company is good, and above average future performance can be extrapolated, then the chances are excellent that you can push for a top P/E ratio.

Because the offering will take months to prepare, the company is vulnerable to the effects of changing business conditions during the interim. It is dangerous for you to try to "time" your offering to just preceed a period of slower growth or a business turndown. The offering could be unavoidably delayed for a myriad of reasons. Any business problem that arises, irrespective of how well it is explained or rationalized, can have a very serious impact upon the P/E ratio, the price of the stock, and the offering itself.

Book Value Per Share

The concept of *book value (or equity) per share* must be given some consideration when undertaking an IPO. By definition, book value is determined by dividing the amount of shareholders' equity to which each share is entitled, by the number of shares outstanding. Shareholders' equity (sometimes referred to as "net worth"), is the sum of the company's assets minus the sum of its liabilities, as reflected on the books of the company. If a company has more than one class of stock outstanding, say both a preferred stock and a common stock, the liquidation rights (value) of the preferred stock must first be deducted from the total shareholders' equity before the book value of the common stock is calculated.

Dilution Incurred by Public Investors

The negotiated offering price of the stock will almost certainly be significantly higher than the calculated net tangible book value per share of the company. One of the disclosures that must be included in the registration statement and prospectus is the amount of dilution incurred by the public investors who purchase the stock at the initial offering price. This dilution is the difference between the public offering price and the pro forma net tangible book value after the offering. If the amount of dilution is significant, say 50 percent or more, the front of the prospectus must include a prominent statement such as: "The Securities Offered Hereby Involve A High Degree Of Risk. See 'Risk Factors' And 'Dilution'."

The following is an example of the type of disclosure which must be made to reflect such dilution. Assume that the company has shareholders' equity of $3 million before the offering. On the basis of the 500,000 shares then outstanding, the pro forma net book value per share is $6.00 ($3,000,000 ÷ 500,000). If a 265,000 share offering is made at $22.00 per share, netting the company $5,030,000 after deducting the costs of the offering, the new shareholders' equity is then $8,030,000. With 765,000 shares now outstanding, the book value per share is $10.50 ($8,030,000 ÷ 765,000). The following dilution summary must be reported in the registration statement and prospectus:

Public offering price		$22.00
Pro forma net tangible book value before offering	$6.00	
Increase per share attributable to public investors	4.50	
Pro forma net tangible book value after offering		10.50
Dilution of net tangible book value to public investors		$11.50

Return on Equity

Book value is an artificially calculated amount and bears no relationship to market value, replacement value, or liquidation value. Usually, a company is worth more than the book value because items such as buildings, machinery, and equipment are reported at their depreciated values. In addition, the value of trademarks, goodwill, engineering designs, and other intangible assets are often not reflected on the books.

Even though its meaningfulness as a financial number is limited, the concept of book value persists as a tool of valuation for the financial community. It is frequently used as a basis of performance measurement through the calculation of the company's return on equity. The return on equity is computed by dividing earnings per share by book value per share. In the preceding example, pre-offering earnings per share were $1.68 and the net book value per share was $6.00, which yields a return on equity of 28% ($1.68 ÷ $6.00). How the company's return on equity compares to other public companies in the same or similar businesses will be a factor in negotiating the P/E ratio and stock price used for the offering. Because the influx of proceeds from the offering will cause an increase in the book value per share, there will be a proportionate decrease in the return on equity until such time as the new capital is employed to expand the earnings of the company.

6

Mechanics of the
Underwriting Syndicate

EACH IBF HAS ITS OWN STRENGTHS AND WEAKNESSES IN WHAT IT CAN or will do for your company. Some IBFs are recognized for their records of success in IPOs for companies in a wide variety of industries, while others have built their reputation primarily with new high-tech companies. Some are better known for the work they do in debt offerings, mergers, and acquisition activities on behalf of extremely large international companies and industry leaders. Still others are more closely associated with highly speculative stock offerings by relatively small and untested companies.

The Purchasing Syndicate

Quite often, the IBF selected by the company going public will invite other IBFs to join with it in underwriting the stock issue. This action forms a temporary group known as the *purchasing syndicate*, and its primary purpose is to spread the risks of underwriting. The addition of some prestigious IBFs to the list of underwriters can help immensely in gaining favorable market acceptance of the offering. Many IBFs have informal understandings with several of their peers regarding regular participation in offerings that any of them originate.

The IBF selected by the company usually functions as the *managing (or lead) underwriter* of the purchasing syndicate and is authorized by the other IBFs to act in their behalf regarding most matters in the subject offering. The members of the purchasing syndicate prepare and execute among themselves a contract called an *agreement among underwriters*. This agreement sets forth the duties and responsibilities of the parties as well as when and how the syndicate will terminate its existence. Each member of the syndicate receives a share of the underwriter's commission (or "spread") proportionate to his participation. The *managing underwriter* receives extra compensation from the other syndicate members for his services.

The Marketing Syndicate

In addition to a purchasing syndicate, a marketing syndicate or "selling group" may be formed by the managing underwriter. The objective of the marketing syndicate is to sell the securities quickly to customers who will hold the stock for investment. It is important that the stock be initially sold to investors who will not soon liquidate their positions and thereby put pressure on the price of the stock immediately after the offering goes on the market. IBFs differ in their marketing strengths. Some firms are very strong in so-called "retail" distribution with many local offices throughout the country selling to the average public investor. Others deal more extensively with big institutional investors (insurance, pension, or mutual fund managers).

Most marketing syndicates function on one of two bases. One is the "firm subscription," wherein each participant is advised in advance of the amount held in reserve for him, and he has the right to make a firm subscription for that fixed number of shares on the offering date. In the other type, the participants are invited to ask for as much as they want, subject to final allocation by the manager. The managing underwriter usually "runs the book" on the offering, meaning he tracks the subscriptions or makes the allocations.

The members of the marketing syndicate prepare and execute a "selling group agreement" among themselves, setting forth the duties and responsibilities of the parties as well as when and how the syndicate will terminate its existence. A portion of the underwriters' compensation goes to the members of the marketing syndicate as a commission for selling the stock. Members of the purchasing syndicate can also be invited to be members of the marketing syndicate, as can other IBFs with strong marketing and distribution capabilities.

Obviously, you will want to select a managing underwriter with an excellent reputation and able to organize a strong syndicate of underwriters.

Is There a Target Investor for Your Stock?

Strong institutional interest in your stock is generally desirable, as institutions usually commit to buy relatively large blocks of stock from the underwriters before the actual stock sale takes place. They are also supposed to be patient investors, interested in the long-term potential of a company. Depending upon the type of business or industry in which your company is engaged, institutions may express significantly less interest in your stock than you might hope for. Some institutions will not even consider a company for investment if the company does not pay a regular dividend.

An IPO that is overwhelmingly dependent upon a successful retail marketing effort can be somewhat more risky for you in terms of achieving your offering objectives. Because the average individual retail sale is much smaller than the large blocks purchased by institutions, many more buyers are required to completely sell out an offering. Your company may have to pay a higher commission (or discount) to the underwriters to be used as an extra incentive for the salespeople in the marketing syndicate to "push" your offering.

Some small underwriting firms might expect you to "pre-sell" a significant portion of your proposed offering by supplying them qualified sales leads—friends, relatives, suppliers, and customers who could be approached to buy shares at the offering. This request is usually a sign of a weak underwriter and a weak marketing syndicate. If most of the underwriters you are interviewing are making such demands, then your company's offering will probably generate limited investor interest and presents a difficult marketing task for the managing underwriter and his syndicate. If this is the case, you may have to reconsider or postpone the effort until you have a quality public offering.

When interviewing a prospective managing underwriter, you should discuss in detail the type of investor to which your company's stock would appeal, the appropriate marketing syndicate to reach that type of investor, and whether that underwriter has a record of successes in putting together the correct syndicate for your type of stock. Have the underwriter document the claims he makes.

7

Finding the Right Underwriter for Your Company

BECAUSE THE PROCESS OF SELLING THE TYPICAL INITIAL STOCK OF-
fering is more or less standardized throughout the investment industry
(no matter what the investment bankers might say), selecting the right
IBF is difficult. You can obtain names of potential underwriters from
sources such as your attorneys, accountants, bankers, and other
professional advisors. While you don't want to "shop around"
excessively, you do want to make as thorough an evaluation of the
various possibilities as you can. Talk to at least four or five IBFs before
you even consider making a preliminary decision. You should tell each
one that others are being considered. If they ask you which others,
tell them—it might be both surprising and helpful to find out what they
have to say about one another.

A relationship with an IBF is not necessarily a marriage made in
heaven, where the parties are tightly bound to one another through
affection, loyalty, and respect. At the very best, the relationship is based
on straightforward business objectives. For the IBF, those objectives
include the earning of underwriting commissions and discounts, the
prestige of being the managing underwriter of a new stock offering
by a quality company, the ability to supply its clientele of institutional
and private investors with new investment possibilities, and the need
to continue to attract client companies that may require additional IBF

services in the future. These services include acquisition and merger activities, and sales of bonds, debentures, and other debt issues.

Forewarned Is Forearmed

IBFs underwrite all the time and know in advance the questions you are going to ask. They give very professional sales pitches that can be deceptively flattering to you, while at the same time creating an aura of awe and mystery about what they do and how they do it. As a newcomer to the business of Wall Street, you can very easily become somewhat overwhelmed and made to feel defensive by the jargon, the players, and the process itself. While your attorneys, accountants, and directors can and should provide advice and support, you need to remain on top of the situation and involved in the meetings and negotiations. You should also expect that your participation in the underwriting process will impact on the time you can devote to managing the day-to-day affairs of the business. A financial consultant, experienced in negotiating and dealing with IBFs, can be of immense value to you.

A primary consideration in the selection of a managing underwriter is demonstrated willingness and ability to provide aftermarket support for stocks they have previously taken public. This support takes a number of forms. First, and most important, is for the managing underwriter to be a *market-maker* in your stock after the offering, helping to support or stabilize the price of the stock by committing some of their own capital to take significant inventory position in your stock. They should be ready to buy stock for their own account when there are large sellers seeking to dispose of shares, and be a seller of stock when there are buyers around. This function is vital in order to minimize extraordinary gyrations in the price of the stock and provide liquidity for larger shareholders.

You should also expect the managing underwriter to provide *analyst* coverage of your company on an ongoing basis. Do they have a respected staff of research analysts who understand your industry and your company? Will they regularly prepare and distribute information on your company to others in the investment community? Review examples of material they have prepared or sponsored for other companies they have taken public.

You might be greatly tempted to automatically choose the biggest, most prestigious underwriter that expresses interest in managing your offering. While on the surface that may sound like a great opportunity, it can be a double-edged sword. The stock offering is a very big step for your company, but on a relative basis, it may be too small a deal for a large IBF to give it the level of attention it deserves and needs, especially in terms of aftermarket support.

Checking Out the Underwriters

During the interviews, prospective underwriters will probably provide you with a list of offerings over the last few years in which they were the managing underwriter and/or a member of the underwriting syndicate. Review the list very carefully, noting such factors as the type and size of the companies involved, how many were IPOs, the per-share price and aggregate dollar value of the offering, and what fees, expenses and commissions were paid to the underwriters in each case. Request a copy of the prospectus for each of the offerings that might be similar to your situation in terms of industry, dollar value of offering, and/or number of shares. When you receive those prospectuses, inspect them carefully, noting the participation level of all underwriting syndicate members, the type and description of the agreement between the company and the underwriters, the expenses incurred by the company in the connection with the offering, etc.

You should then call the senior executive of several of those companies, identify yourself, and ask for any comments regarding the performance of the managing underwriter before, during, and after the offering process. Ask straight out if he or she has any suggestions or cautions for you as you begin the process. You will find that most of the executives will be glad to help you, but will be a bit embarrassed to admit that they made any mistakes in judgment. Be sensitive to that point and phrase your questions carefully. Specific questions you should ask are:

- How did the per-share price actually received for the stock compare to the per-share price they were led to expect earlier in the negotiations with the managing underwriter? Ask for an explanation of any difference.

- What happened to the price of the stock over the six weeks following the offering? Was there a significant increase or decrease? If so, what was the reason?

- Has the managing underwriter's research analysts visited the company and published follow-up reports and favorable recommendations? Has the underwriter recently sponsored any meetings or conferences at which the company's officers could make a presentation to stimulate investment interest in the company's stock?

- If the company had to do it all over again, would it select the same managing underwriter? If not, why not?

Due Diligence

You should also be aware that during the time you are evaluating the candidates for managing underwriter, they will probably be investigating and evaluating you, your management team, and your company's history and reputation regarding products, quality, engineering, fiscal responsibility, and integrity. This process, referred to as *due diligence* is a necessary and legally required function of the underwriter and his professional staff. To some degree, the thoroughness and depth of a due diligence review performed by a candidate underwriter is an indicator of his seriousness in being your underwriter and the quality of his underwriting effort. They probably will talk to customers, suppliers and industry sources.

Full disclosure of any significant negative past events or situations is necessary. Lawsuits, bankruptcies, revocations of professional licenses, criminal records, difficulties with the IRS, etc., involving you, the company, or any of its other officers and directors might have to be disclosed in the prospectus. If you (or anyone on your management team) have any skeletons-in-the-closet, get an opinion from your personal and corporate attorneys. The underwriters' unearthing of damaging information about which you had not been entirely straightforward would be most unfortunate. Even if they do not discover it, if information that should have been disclosed in the prospectus comes out at a later date, serious civil and/or criminal penalties could be imposed if circumstances warrant.

Making the Final Selection

Assuming that all the tangible factors are more or less equal among the underwriting candidates, select the largest firm having personnel with whom you have been able to work well and feel comfortable. Often, the underwriter's representative who "sells" the firm to you is not the person with whom you'll do the most work later. Ask to meet the key workers who will be assigned to your offering. There will be a lot of stress and strain during the underwriting process, and good "personal chemistry" among the participants helps considerably.

When you feel that you and your advisors have reached a conclusion as to the IBF you would prefer for managing underwriter, don't be too quick to cut off communications with the others. You and your underwriter of choice must first resolve the very critical elements addressed in the next three chapters:

- Type of underwriting

- Pricing the stock

- Underwriters' compensation

8

What Kind of Deal?

IN MOST NORMAL UNDERWRITING SITUATIONS, YOU AND THE UNDER-writer are under no legal commitment to go through with the deal until, literally, a few hours before the actual offering takes place and the formal *underwriting agreement* is signed by your company and the managing underwriter.

Read the Fine Print

While your company and the underwriter might have earlier signed a *letter of intent* or other document outlining the proposed details and terms of the future offering, the letter or document will state that portions of it are only a tentative understanding and are not binding on either party. The underwriting agreement usually contains a "market out" clause which permits the underwriter to cancel its obligations under a wide variety of contingencies.

From the underwriter's viewpoint, there are a number of sound reasons for that practice: the SEC might not clear your registration statement in time for the public offering; when your offering is ready to go, the stock market might be too weak to support the number of shares or the per-share price originally contemplated; or perhaps while the registration work is being completed, your business goes into a severe slump, adversely impacting its future prospects and thus the marketability of the stock offering. No underwriter wants to be "on the hook" to perform when situations over which he has no control can change several months hence.

As part of the underwriter selection process, you must reach a clear understanding on the type of underwriting, pricing of the stock, and the underwriters' compensation. Unless certain difficulties or problems arise, most reputable underwriters will honor the arrangements as first set out in the terms of the letter of intent or other document. Your company will also be expected to fulfill its responsibilities and go through with the transaction, unless something serious and unexpected happens. Under normal circumstances, you should expect the formal underwriting agreement to contain the same terms, conditions, and arrangements as the earlier, letter of intent.

Types of Underwriting Contracts

"Type of underwriting" refers to the nature of the formal, binding commitment between the underwriters and the company regarding the purchase/sale of the stock offering. This commitment is entered into only after all the necessary SEC and other legal clearances have been obtained. An underwriting generally falls into one of two classes:

- *Firm Commitment Underwriting*—The underwriters agree to buy from the company (and from any selling shareholders) all the stock being offered, at a fixed price. If unable to find sufficient buyers for all the stock, the underwriters must buy the unsold portion, hold it for their own account, and sell it when they can in the future.

- *Best Efforts Underwriting*—The underwriters only agree to use their "best efforts" to sell all the stock in the offering. If unable to sell all the stock, the underwriters are not committed to purchase the unsold portion as they are under the firm commitment agreement. There are several variations on the "best efforts" underwriting, the two most common are:

  - *All-or-None Underwriting*—The underwriters agree to use their "best efforts" to sell all the stock. If unable to sell all the stock, none is considered sold, and the offering is cancelled.

- *Minimum Percentage Underwriting*—The underwriters agree to use their "best efforts" to sell all the stock. If a certain pre-set minimum percentage of the shares is sold (say 50% or 75%, etc.), then the offering is considered accomplished. The underwriters have no obligation to purchase the unsold portion.

Think It Over Carefully

The firm commitment is the most desirable underwriting arrangement for the company because, once the formal underwriting contract is signed, you know that you will get the agreed-upon sum of money at the closing of the offering. This is the type of commitment you should seek during your interviews and negotiations with the candidate underwriting firms.

If your company is considered a very speculative investment, you might not get a firm commitment. If you insist upon a per-share offering price or P/E ratio that the underwriter considers excessive for the market, or if the feedback from his marketing efforts indicates weak interest in your stock, a best efforts commitment might be the only alternative offered.

Accepting a best efforts arrangement compounds the risks involved in any stock offering. You shouldn't automatically turn it down if it is your only option, but you do need to assess the various ramifications of a best efforts offering very closely:

- Is your company's financial condition such that you can (or want to) wait for a surer deal?

- Will you accept a significantly lower offering price to make the stock an "easier sell"?

- Are you willing to accept lower total proceeds if all the stock cannot be sold?

- Are you so anxious to raise money that the type of underwriting doesn't matter? Have you no acceptable alternatives?

If you settle for some form of best-efforts/minimum-percentage arrangement, you might find that enough stock is sold to leave you with all the reporting requirements and unique expenses of a public company, but not the total amount of money you really need and want.

If you accept a best-efforts/all-or-none arrangement, at least you won't go public unless all the stock is sold and all the proceeds received.

Generally speaking, the larger underwriting firms will agree to a firm commitment only with a quality company having normal speculative characteristics. The best efforts arrangement is more common when dealing with smaller underwriting firms, especially when the company seeking to go public is highly speculative, relatively new and untested by time, or lesser in over-all quality than its peer companies.

Your opinion of your company might be quite different from the investment community's opinion. If you use the services of a financial consultant experienced in Wall Street matters, and have discussed your potential offering with a reasonable number of IBFs, a consensus of opinion will develop. You must be realistic in your expectations. The type of deal you can obtain is probably more dependent upon the mood on Wall Street and the attractiveness of your company as an investment than on the specific firm you select as underwriter.

9

Pricing the Stock

PRICING THE STOCK INVOLVES A COMBINATION OF JUDGMENT, NEGO-
tiating skills, luck, timing, and simple mathematics.

The Complex Pricing Recipe

To start with, the number of shares outstanding and the number
of new shares to be sold by the company will obviously have an influence
on the market value of each individual share. Whatever the total market
value of the company is determined to be, the more shares of stock
representing that value, the lower in value (price) each individual share
will be.

The amount of money the company is attempting or willing to raise
via the stock offering also affects the pricing. Most of the midsize or
larger underwriters prefer an offering that totals at least $5 million.
From your standpoint, you should try for the largest aggregate offering
you can get. One reason is the principle stressed earlier—getting the
most money you can when money is available to you. Another reason
is the significant legal, accounting, printing, and other costs, you will
incur in connection with the offering. These costs can be considered
fixed costs, because they should be (but often are not) unrelated to

the aggregate dollar value of the offering. Thus, the larger the offering, the less each dollar of new capital should cost you.

To appeal to the largest potential marketplace, most underwriters generally prefer the issue to be in the $10- to $25-per-share price range. Many of the larger potential investors, especially financial institutions, associate a stock price below $10 per share with a lack of quality, and might not even consider it for purchase. The average individual investor, who usually buys stock in 100-share lots, prefers a price less than $25 per share so that his aggregate investment in a stock does not represent a major commitment of his personal capital. Neither position has anything to do with the quality of your company or its worth; it is just a peculiarity of stock market psychology with which you must contend.

A sufficient number of shares must be offered to achieve wide distribution at the initial stock sale and provide support for an active aftermarket. Generally speaking, an offering of at least 400,000 shares is the minimum to reach those objectives. The overall size of the offering can be increased if any of the current shareholders want to sell some of their holdings in connection with the company's offering. An IPO in which many of the shares being sold are from current shareholders can create an unfavorable impression for the public and the underwriter. This situation can give the appearance of a *bailout* and a lack of confidence in the future of the company by those most familiar with the company.

Most underwriters are highly reputable professionals and do their utmost to serve the interests of you, their client. Even the best underwriter, however, faces conflicting pressures, and you must not be naive about this when you negotiate with him. Although you will pay the underwriter compensation in the form of a cash commission or cash discount calculated as a percentage (7-10 percent) of the stock selling price, for every dollar of stock price concession you agree to, the underwriter loses very little of his revenue compared to what you lose in proceeds. Because one of his primary functions is to sell stock to investors, it is easier for the underwriter to sell a stock that is somewhat underpriced relative to its true value than one that is fully priced. Underwriters also depend upon repeat business from the individuals and institutions to whom they sell the stock. These buyers want winners, stocks that will go up in value after the initial offering. All other things being equal, an underpriced offering has the better chance of going up.

Although you are initially seeking to negotiate the highest possible price for your stock, you can and should back off from that price somewhat to help ensure a well-received offering, and you can anticipate that the underwriter will probably suggest this shortly before the offering is made. Most underwriting firms believe that company owners think their company is worth considerably more than its actual value and find this subject to be the most difficult and sensitive to negotiate. As long as you know beforehand what the realistic and fair value of the stock is, you can make whatever concessions your good judgment tells you are necessary.

Know Where You Stand Before You Start

By and large, the starting point for determining the market value of your company is the comparison of its operational and financial performance and status with that of publicly owned companies engaged in the same or similar businesses. If there are several publicly owned, peer-group companies in the market, then the investment community has already determined what it is willing to pay in your industry for a given level of performance, growth, and potential.

In preparing for an underwriting, you should accumulate a complete dossier, including annual and quarterly reports to shareholders and prospectuses (if any), on every public company that is a direct competitor or engaged in the same business, or in a very similar business, as yours. For each of them, prepare an analysis indicating:

- annual sales,
- profit as a percentage of sales,
- return on equity,
- book value,
- shares outstanding,
- earnings per share,
- market price of stock,
- total market valuation,
- price/earnings ratio,
- and any other factors which can be used as a basis for comparison with similar data on your company.

This information will help you arrive at an initial valuation of your company and can provide you with valuable support during your share-price negotiations with the underwriter.

Irrespective of these performance comparisons, timing and luck can have an enormous effect on the price you obtain. Your offering might hit the market during a sudden world crisis (oil embargo, major bank failure, assassination, credit crunch, etc.) that causes stock prices and market values to go haywire. Or, perhaps, a few stock offerings of companies similar to yours have just taken place, or are ready to take place, and adversely impact on the market's interest in your issue. The possibilities are almost endless, and most of them will have a negative impact on your offering.

10

The Underwriter's Compensation

YOUR MAJOR COST ITEM IN GOING PUBLIC WILL PROBABLY BE THE compensation paid to the underwriters. The commission or discount you will be charged is one of the key elements that you should negotiate strongly with the lead underwriter, and underwriters can and do request other forms of additional compensation.

No Free Lunch

In assessing how much bargaining room you have, you must be realistic. There are no "steals" or "super bargains." No matter how good a negotiator you are, the best you can expect to end up with is a fair deal. Quality companies making a quality offering through a quality underwriter can, in normal market conditions, expect to pay the current average commission or discount, without any extra compensation or onerous terms in the deal. If you change any part of the "quality" equation—company, offering, underwriter, or market conditions—then you can expect more expensive terms.

The *National Association of Securities Dealers* (NASD), is a self-regulating association of brokers and dealers in the *over-the-counter* (OTC) market. While one of its functions is to review the reasonableness of the direct and indirect compensation paid to underwriters, you should not rely upon that organization to protect you from your own poor business judgment or lack of experience in underwriting matters.

Do Your Homework First

During your early interviews, the various underwriting candidates should have given you lists of offerings they have managed or participated in. Using the prospectuses for those offerings, prepare an analysis of each offering, indicating the following information:

- Aggregate dollar value of the offering

- Number of shares offered

- Underwriting commissions and discounts, expressed as a dollar amount per share and/or as a percentage of the offering price

- Type of underwriting commitment—firm or best efforts

- Underwriter's expense allowance, if any, paid or reimbursed by the company

- Supplementary compensation, if any, paid to the underwriter through an earlier sale of stock to the underwriter at a price below the offering price or in the form of options or *warrants* which permit the underwriter to purchase company stock at a predetermined and favorable fixed price for a number of years

- Other undesirable conditions, such as giving the underwriter the right of first refusal to handle the company's future offerings, the right to a seat on the board of directors, or an ongoing retainer for consulting

- Expenses (legal, accounting, printing, and filing fees, etc.) incurred by the company in connection with the offering

These analyses will give you a picture of recent trends for the various types, sizes, and qualities of offerings. You can expect that each underwriter will initially propose terms that are a bit more expensive than, but fairly consistent with, what they received in other offerings of a similar nature to yours. You should also find that the terms proposed to you by the various underwriters are quite similar to one another. In fact, be suspicious of any proposal that falls at either extreme, high or low. Tell them that they are outside the range you had expected and ask them to justify their position. Don't reject them out of hand; listen carefully to their rationale and apply what they explain to you in your evaluation of all the proposals.

An underwriter incurs a certain level of fixed costs no matter what the size of the offering. Initially, an underwriter earns revenues through commission or discount rate. If your offering is relatively small, the commission or discount rate will tend to be high in order to meet the underwriter's revenue budget. Unless an underwriter is going to provide some special, desirable services which, during the interviews, were not generally considered part of any underwriter's normal functions, fight any request for an additional expense allowance. If you must agree to it, insist that it be payable only after a successful offering, and that the underwriter be accountable for it and provide documentation to support claims for reimbursement.

Watch Out for the Extras

Certain forms of underwriter's compensation are frequently associated with offerings of a below-average quality or highly speculative nature. Such offerings typically have a relatively high commission or discount rate for the underwriters. In addition, the company, in advance of the offering, may have to agree to sell a certain number of shares to the underwriter at a bargain price, well below the price at which the offering is ultimately made. Sometimes, the underwriter will try to obtain options or warrants to purchase shares at a fixed and predetermined favorable price. These options or warrants can be exercised or resold any time after the offering, and can reap very handsome rewards for the underwriter if the price of the stock goes up after the offering. Both of these types of "goodies" offer underwriters ways to considerably increase their compensation for handling risky offerings.

The proposed underwriting agreement might also obligate the company to use the same underwriter for the next public offering made by the company, if any. This can tie the hands of the company if it needs a bigger, better, or stronger underwriter for the next offering. Sometime in the future, the company might need to "buy its way" out of that commitment, and this can be expensive or impossible. Refuse to agree to any such formal condition. At most, you should agree to include the underwriter in your list of candidates when and if another offering takes place.

Some underwriters like to have one or more guaranteed seats on the company's board of directors. While the company can often benefit from the business knowledge and experience of such board members, the company is better off not bound to such a condition. If the shareholders and management believe that a representative of the underwriter can make a positive contribution to the growth and prosperity of the company, they can voluntarily invite the underwriter's participation on the board.

As undesirable as most of the above conditions are, they might be necessary for you to get an underwriter to manage your offering. If the negotiations with all the candidate underwriters seem to be moving in that direction, you are either not talking to quality firms, or your company's situation leaves a great deal to be desired. More than likely, you are also only being offered a risky best efforts arrangement. In this case you should decide whether to go public under these circumstances or wait until you can qualify for better underwriting terms.

You might be able to do considerably better than the norm in negotiating the commission or discount rate and should be able to avoid the various types of extra underwriter's compensation if your company and its management:

- are widely respected for a strong marketing and technology position,
- are in an industry which has current investment appeal,
- reflect a history of consistently good sales and earnings growth,
- have done the preparatory public relations work to pre-sell your favorable image,
- are making a large enough offering, and
- can be considered a "feather in the cap" of any underwriter who gets your account.

"Considerably better" probably means a reduction of only 10-20 percent off the rate paid by the average company with an offering the size of yours. But a reduction in rate from 9% to 7½% on an offering of $5,000,000 still can save you $75,000, and avoidance of the extra compensation can save you significantly more.

A Word of Warning

Some underwriting firms, usually smaller organizations, have engaged in practices that border on the unethical. One of their tactics is to negotiate for an upfront, unaccountable expense allowance in cash (usually expressed in the form of a small percentage of the aggregate proposed offering value) at the time the "letter of intent" is signed. They then proceed to do nothing of any value. Their inaction is disguised by a flurry of phone calls, pointless meetings, and other tactics designed to mislead the business owner into thinking that something is really happening. Meanwhile, the owner is spending additional thousands of dollars with the company's accountants and attorneys getting ready to prepare the registration statement. After a few months, when most of the unaccountable expense allowance has been collected from the business owner, the underwriter will sadly report that he is unable to do the deal because of market conditions, weak investor interest in your company, or any number of other excuses. You are left high and dry, with as much as $100,000 in legal and accounting fees already spent, not to mention the $10,000 to $20,000 paid to the underwriter.

11

The Timetable and Registration Statement

WHEN YOU HAVE CONCLUDED YOUR ARRANGEMENTS WITH THE UN-
derwriter and selected the attorneys and accountants you will use, all
the participants must get together as soon as possible for a master
planning session to establish a timetable and assign responsibilities.
Usually referred to as an *all hands meeting*, this meeting should include
company officers, staff, and consultants who will be participating in
the registration process; company attorneys and independent
accountants; and the underwriter and his attorneys.

The objective of the all hands meeting is to list each significant
step to be accomplished in the registration process and for each one:

- estimate the time it will require,
- assign a starting and completion date,
- decide which of the participants are primarily responsible for
  its satisfactory completion,
- determine whose assistance or inputs will be required and when,
  and
- arrange for whatever other resources are needed.

Time Is Really Money Now

The date that the registration statement is first filed and the date it finally becomes effective will determine the date(s) of the financial statements required to be in the registration statement. This is an extremely important matter and deserves careful planning and attention. If too long a period elapses between the two dates, the financial data will be considered stale, and the SEC or the underwriter will insist that you provide more current financial statements for the final registration statement and prospectus. This can be very expensive and time consuming. Therefore, the timetable should be developed and coordinated with the availability of the necessary financial statements in mind. Strong consideration should be given to establishing and sticking to a schedule which will permit the use of the year-end audited financial statements to satisfy all the financial information requirements.

To maintain this timetable, at the first planning session you must determine the availability of all the participants and decision makers throughout the schedule (vacations, travel plans, other personal commitments, etc.), the potential impact of delayed responses from other organizations (e.g., another company, the U.S. Government, a foreign entity or government, etc.) providing necessary data or documentation, and any other factor which could adversely impact the schedule.

Sometimes the personnel assigned by the professional firms to participate in the preparation of the registration statement do not have the full authority to make decisions on various matters that will come up while the work is in progress. This can be very frustrating and re-sult in unnecessary delays, especially as the work draws to a conclusion and time starts getting short. While this cannot always be avoided, you should mention your concerns on this subject at the first meeting.

On a regular and frequent basis, the progress of each participant and the status of each item on the master schedule must be validated and compared to what was planned. This important function must be specifically assigned to one of the participants, preferably you or your chief financial officer. Any deviations from the timetable must be assessed in terms of their short-term and long-term impact on meeting the target filing date. The interdependency and sequential nature of many of the items can have a serious downstream effect if delays are not recognized and dealt with promptly. Everyone should be kept abreast of the current situation and, if necessary, be brought together to review or revise the timetable or assignments.

One of the risks when you start the process of going public is the possibility of one or more unforeseen business or personal events arising that could have an adverse effect upon the key members of the executive team or the company itself. The longer it takes to complete the offering, the longer the company remains exposed to internal and external events which could delay or kill the offering entirely. You must be careful that the original timetable is as tight as possible and that everyone sticks to it. You cannot afford to be a passive bystander and let the schedule slip. Be as involved and insistent as you possibly can, because you have the most to lose if things go awry.

Contents of the Registration Statement

The federal law that governs the offer and sale of securities is primarily a disclosure statute, requiring that the public be given sufficient information about the company to make an informed decision about investment in its securities. The law does not require that the offering be favorable to the investors or that the company (or its officers and directors) be successful in its business endeavors. Full and clear disclosure of all pertinent and substantive matters must be made, and this requirement is subject to hindsight judgment in the event a problem arises in the future.

The SEC has two primary regulations regarding the filing of forms under the *Securities Act of 1933* and the *Securities Exchange Act of 1934*. These are *Regulation S-X*, which sets forth the requirements for financial statements required to be filed as part of the registration statement, and *Regulation S-K*, which states the requirements applicable to the non-financial-statement portions of the registration statement.

The registration statement filed with the SEC is made up of two main parts:

Part I—The prospectus, usually bound separately and distributed to members of the public and the investment community who are being offered the shares for purchase (see Appendix). Although your attorneys and underwriter will know the exact prospectus requirements for your offering, a typical prospectus includes the following sections:

- Front Cover—Date of the prospectus, description of the offering and securities, number of shares and offering price, underwriting discounts and commissions, and proceeds to the company. If the offering is considered highly speculative, the cover should contain an appropriate and prominently placed notice.

- Prospectus Summary—Includes brief descriptions of the company, its business, and the securities being offered. The amount and use of proceeds is given, along with a summary of certain financial information. Significant risk factors must also be set out separately.

- The Company—Brief description of the primary business activities, where and when incorporated, and location of its principal offices.

- Risk Factors—Any significant factors that make the offering a high-risk or speculative one must be disclosed and explained here. Examples include an offering in which there is material dilution to the public investors as a result of the offering, potential dilution due to outstanding warrants or options, a lack of business experience or earnings history, dependence on a limited number of customers or suppliers, reliance upon an unproven technology, product, or market, etc.

- Dilution—Any material dilution of the public investors' equity interest resulting from the difference between the tangible book value per share before the offering and the offering price.

- Use of Proceeds—How and for what the company intends to use the proceeds of the offering. If there is no specific plan for using the proceeds, that fact must be disclosed.

- Dividend Policy—What the company's dividend history has been, what its present policy is, and any restirctions on paying dividends. If the company intends to reinvest future earnings instead of paying dividends, it must so indicate.

- Capitalization—Sets forth the company's debt (if any) and stockholders' equity both before and after the offering, giving the effect of the use of proceeds if one of the stated purposes was to reduce debt.

- Selected Financial Data—A summary of certain financial information for the last five years and the interim period, if any, since the last year end (and the comparative interim period of the preceding year). As a minimum, sales or operating revenue, profit or loss (in total and on a per-share basis), and certain balance sheet data are given.

- Management's Discussion and Analysis—Usually in narrative form, this section provides information on cash flow, liquidity, capital resources, and results of operations. Trends, commitments, or situations which have affected or might affect sales, revenues, operating results, working capital, or capital expenditures are explained for each of the last three years plus any interim periods reported.

- Description of the Business—An in-depth synopsis of the company's business operations. Topics covered include:

  - a history of the company (with special concentration on the last five years),
  - principal products or services,
  - principal markets, methods of marketing and distribution,
  - competitive situation,
  - revenue, operating profit or loss, and assets by major industry segment and by geographic area (if appropriate),
  - research and development in the last three years,
  - details regarding patents, trademarks, licenses, franchises, and concessions held,
  - dependence upon one (or a few) large customers,
  - source and availability of raw materials or components,
  - dollar amount of firm backlog,
  - seasonal factors, if any,
  - government contracts,
  - export sales and activities,
  - special working capital requirements dictated by the business,
  - information regarding employees, including number of employees, labor relations, and special education or skill requirements, and
  - government regulation and environmental matters.

- Properties—Location and description of principal physical properties owned or leased.

- Legal Proceedings—Disclosure of any pending legal proceedings considered *material* to the offering.

- Management and Certain Security Holders—

  - Background information about management personnel and major stockholders (including age, business experience, compensation, options, perquisites, employment agreements, and severance arrangements).
  - Loans made by the company to (and certain transactions with) major stockholders, directors, and management personnel (including their immediate families)
  - Stock holdings of all officers, directors, and any persons who beneficially own more than five percent of any class of stocks
  - Transactions with promoters, if the company has been in existence for less than five years.

- Description of Securities—The title, par or stated value, dividend rights, voting rights, and conversion, liquidation, or pre-emptive rights of the securities being offered and all classes of stock. The terms and conditions of any warrants or rights offered or outstanding are also described.

- Underwriter Information—Explains the plan of distribution for the offering, including the names of participants in the underwriting syndicate, the number of shares underwritten by each firm and the method of underwriting (e.g., best efforts), the underwriters' compensation, indemnification, and material relationships with the company.

- Legal Matters—Identifies the attorneys who are rendering opinions on the securities for both the company and the underwriters and discloses any of the attorneys' shareholdings in the company.

- Experts—Identifies any experts who have been relied upon in the preparation of the registration statement (e.g., the independent accountants).

- Additional Information—Refers to the availability of additional information filed under Part II below, and the address where copies of said material can be obtained.

- Financial Statements—Form S-1 registration requires audited balance sheets as of the end of the last two fiscal years, audited statements of income, changes in financial position, and stockholders' equity for the last three fiscal years. If the registration statement will not become effective within 135 days after the end of the company's fiscal year, then the unaudited interim statements covering quarters subsequent to the latest fiscal year must also be provided, along with comparative unaudited interim statements for the preceding year.

Part II—Supplemental information that is generally not distributed to the public, but is available for public examination at the offices of the SEC including:

- copies of various corporate documents (articles of incorporation, charter, by-laws, etc.) and contracts (stock option plan, pension plan, key executive employment contracts, etc.,

- details regarding any sales of unregistered securities for the last three years,

- other expenses of issuance and distribution of the offering,

- indemnification of directors and officers,

- certain financial schedules, and

- the underwriting agreement.

If the business, technology, or activities of the company are highly technical and complex, matters must be described in enough detail so that a layman can understand the company's product or service and the purposes which it will serve. A glossary in the prospectus, to define and explain any technical terms, might be appropriate.

The full and complete disclosure of all material and potentially material information in a very clear, non-misleading manner is the collective responsibility of the company, its officers, accountants, and attorneys as well as the underwriter and his legal counsel. The prospectus has a number of conflicting objectives which can cause considerable friction among the various participants during its preparation. You might want the prospectus to sound more optimistic and less conservative than the way it has been written and may waste time and money attempting to convince the attorneys to be more aggressive in the presentation. But it is not in their best interests to do so, and frankly, it is not important enough to fight about. Traditionally, most, if not all, prospectuses reflect a conservative approach. Those investors who read prospectuses are used to that. From a potential legal liability standpoint, a complete and totally factual prospectus is much more important.

12

What Makes
a Good Prospectus?

TO SAY THAT A GOOD PROSPECTUS IS ONE THAT ACCOMPANIED A SUC-
cessful, well-received offering would be a gross oversimplification. The
reality is, most individual investors do not bother to study the
prospectus before buying the stock being offered, and even fewer understand the document. Although the primary purpose of the prospectus
is to fully disclose all pertinent information, data, and risks associated
with an offering, most prospectuses make for rather boring reading,
appealing only to lawyers, accountants, stock brokers, and some careful,
selective investors. As a general rule, however, the institutional investor
and other purchasers of large blocks of stock do read prospectuses very
carefully before committing to buy.

"Why Is This Stock Different from All Other Stocks?"

One of the basic questions a potential investor has when considering
the purchase of stock in an IPO is, what is there about *this* company
that sets it above and apart from other companies in its industry and
the many other investment alternatives I have? If the prospectus can
convey the answer to that question in a simple, direct way, then the
prospectus will not only have satisfied the standard disclosure

requirements, but will have contributed immensely to achieving a successful offering.

SEC rules and restrictions as well as the deliberate conservatism of most attorneys specializing in SEC matters prevent the prospectus from being written in an upbeat or promotional style. Nevertheless, while still meeting the disclosure requirements and legal cautions, some prospectuses are better written than others and do a better job in promoting investor interest in the company.

Paint a Complete Picture

When the prospectus is drafted, make certain that the things that *you* think make the company a good investment are expressed. View the various sections of the prospectus as specific opportunities to explain what is good and unique about your company. Remember that one of the purposes of the various sections is to convey a picture of the entire company; that is, the various sections must "hang together" and support one another. The sections on "Products" and "Product Technology" should interact with one another and with other sections such as "Product Development" or "Patents and Licenses," if appropriate. Exceptionally important factors can be repeated or restated in more than one section for added emphasis. Do not depend upon the legal professionals to either understand what really makes your business successful, or be eager to express that information in the prospectus even if they do understand.

The Appendix contains a reprint of a well-written prospectus issued by Alliant Computer Systems Corporation in connection with an offering of 1,750,000 common shares at $15.00 per share on December 17, 1986. Alliant is in the computer business, along with hundreds of other companies. Their products are highly technical and probably beyond the ken of most investors, yet the prospectus was carefully written to allow the reader to differentiate Alliant's products from those of other computer manufacturers and to comprehend the particular market niche to which Alliant has targeted its product.

Regardless of what your company's business is, the concept of your market niche is an important one to get across to the potential investor. It is the rare company that isn't faced with a myriad of competitors, many of whom are larger, better financed, and more well-known. Showing that your company has the right product targeted at an appropriate market is a major part of the message you are attempting to convey. The Alliant prospectus does an excellent job of both distinguishing its "mini-supercomputer" products from other, perhaps better known computer systems, and identifying the type of market to which its efforts are directed. In the "Business—Background" section of its prospectus, Alliant points out the application and limitation of existing superminicomputers for engineering and scientific computing, the multimillion-dollar cost of the top-end supercomputers, and the advantages of their "mini-supercomputer" products which bridge the price/performance gap between the two. In just a few short paragraphs and with a minimum of technical jargon, Alliant's market niche has been clearly identified and justified.

Many companies going public for the first time have had a relatively short business history. Seemingly untested by time, their image as a sound investment may be hampered. Alliant was able to deal with this problem by using the credibility provided by the name recognition of its customers in its prospectus. Although Alliant was founded in 1982, incurred substantial losses during its developmental stage, and had sold only 54 of its systems since the sale of its first commercial units in late 1985, the listing of most of its 29 customers to date in the "Markets, Applications and Customers" section of the prospectus gives significant support to the viability and potential of the company. The list contains many well-known industrial, research, engineering, and scientific institutions, and provides enormous credibility for the statements made in other routine sections of the prospectus. Thus, while merely stating cold facts, the writers of this prospectus solved a potential image problem and communicated some important "stock promotion" information in a perfectly acceptable manner.

If part of your company's present and future success is dependent upon technology factors, then your prospectus should clearly indicate the "what and how" of your proprietary technology. The "Products" and "Product Technology" sections of the Alliant prospectus help the nontechnical reader understand the nature and purpose of the products. While the "System Hardware" and "System Software" sections are fairly technical and complex for the average reader to really understand, a large number of institutional investors want this type of information and have the technical expertise available to evaluate it before they commit to making a significant investment.

Work with What You Have

Not every company considering an IPO is involved in a high technology business and able to pepper its prospectus with references to digital widgets, systems gadgets, and high-speed what-nots. Nevertheless, the principle of stressing what is unique and positive about your company still holds. Whether your company is a small chain of fast lubrication and oil-change centers, a string of health-care centers for the aged, or a manufacturer of children's clothes, you must get your message across. However, as important as it is to explain how you got to where you are, your prospectus must supply sufficient information, directly or indirectly, as to how you will continue to grow. For example, if your past success was highly dependent upon the geographic location of your retail outlets, you must deal with the obvious question of how the company intends to have additional stores in locations equally as productive. A business that depends upon the continuation of a trend (e.g., the growing population of the aged) must provide the data to substantiate the existence and long-term continuation of that trend. You cannot assume that what is obvious to you in running your business and planning for the future will be as apparent and clearly understood by a potential investor.

While the prospectus accompanying a public offering of stock is a document that dwells on the past and present, in the final analysis, a stock investment is really an investment in the future. You cannot make promises or forecasts in the prospectus, but a well-written prospectus will point to the future. It should provide sufficient factual information to the reader to enable him or her to have a clear vision of what strengths and resources the company has, what future markets are available to the company, and how the company intends to exploit its opportunities. There is no need to gild the lily, but a positive and honest approach to the structure and content of a prospectus is a good strategy.

13

Legal and
Accounting Expenses

SUCCESSFUL BUSINESSMEN INSIST THAT THE VARIOUS EXPENSES OF running their businesses be budgeted, managed, and controlled, however, when it comes to the out-of-pocket expenses connected with a public offering of their securities (especially the IPO), this policy gets lost in the shuffle. Somehow, an attitude develops that "it's the public's money that's going to pay the bills, so who cares."

In an IPO, every dollar you save in professional expenses is a dollar that will stay in the corporate treasury; professional expenses incurred solely in connection with a stock offering are not tax-deductible—they are netted against the capital you raise.

Don't Give a Blank Check

Some attorneys and accountants involved in public offerings, take advantage of the situation by charging fees that are related not to the amount of work to be done in connection with the offering, but rather to the dollar size of the offering itself. Because an IPO is a new experience for the company, management is dealing in an area where it probably has no basis for comparison and might be hesitant to challenge the professionals.

The out-of-pocket expenses for a typical $5 million is about $300,000. Depending upon how well-prepared the company's legal and accounting records were beforehand, the complexity of certain aspects of the company's operations (foreign subsidiaries, government-regulated business, complicated patent rights, etc.), and how much attention management gives to negotiating and controlling these professional expenses, costs can vary widely.

You can do a number of things to hold down the expenses. At the very beginning, make clear to the legal and accounting professionals that you intend to monitor their charges closely. Before they start, have them provide you with a detailed budget, broken down by the hours they expect to spend in each major area of work. The billing rate per hour for each of the different levels of their staff should also be given. Request progress reports over the course of the work, and measure it against the budget. You and/or your chief financial officer can keep your own independent log of the time you have observed the professionals working on your offering. Although you won't know the time they spent on your work while in their offices, it will still give you a reasonable picture of what is going on.

One of the biggest reasons for high professional costs can be the failure of your own employees to have necessary information ready for the professionals when promised. Don't have an attorney or accountant search through your files for $150 an hour, when one of your own employees could have done it for $10 an hour. All the routine corporate legal records should be up to date, in the proper order, and easily located. More time and money will be wasted if simple legal or accounting housekeeping has been ignored for one reason or another.

Qualified Professionals Can Save You Time and Money

As recommended earlier, a CPA firm experienced in working on registration statements will be knowledgeable and efficient in getting the necessary financial information prepared in the appropriate format. Regular annual audits of the company's financial statements will hold down the accounting costs associated with the offering.

If practical, the timing of your offering should be such that the financial information requirements are satisfied by using your normal year-end audited statements. If you use any other interim date, you will incur significantly higher accounting fees because the accountants will have to do much more work reviewing and testing the interim data, even if they do not audit that period. This holds true not only for the current interim period, but for the prior year's data which must be provided for comparison.

Whenever possible, have the members of the company's accounting staff—not the outside accountants—prepare any necessary financial or numeric data. Turn over the completed work and the supporting information to the accountants so that they can limit their work to testing and verification. The partner of the CPA firm need not be present at many of the meetings held with the attorneys. His time is expensive, and he should probably only be there for the initial planning and final approval phases.

The more SEC experience your attorneys have, the better for you and your company. Do not have your regular attorneys responsible for significant portions of the registration statement if they do not have expertise and prior experience in such matters. You should not have to pay for their on-the-job training. Engaging the services of another law firm, one with a respected reputation in SEC registrations, might seem more expensive but will probably save you time and money in the long run.

While the underwriter will assign a law firm of his own choosing and *at his own expense* to work with you and your outside professional staff in the preparation and review of the registration statement, the firm's primary role is to protect its client, the underwriter. Your company is *not* the client of this law firm.

The firm will also review various records and documents of your company (minute books, stock ownership records, corporate charter, bylaws, contracts, leases, patents, etc.) to be certain that everything is in order. This can be an expensive and time-consuming process, especially if your company has been lax in maintaining its records and files. While the underwriter's counsel is not being paid by you, the more that your attorneys have to update the records, make modifications, render opinions, or give lengthy explanations, the greater your legal costs will be. In fact, the sloppier and less professional your records are, the less confidence the underwriter's counsel will have in what he does review; thus, he will tend to review more and more.

You should be on the alert for a clash of egos and styles between your attorneys and the underwriter's counsel. It is not uncommon for a strong, adversarial atmosphere to develop between the professionals, which can only end up making things more difficult and more expensive for you. If and when you see it developing, you should have a private talk with the underwriter to convey your concerns. More than likely, he will speak to his attorneys, as you should to yours, advocating a more cooperative attitude from everyone.

The Prospectus Is a Major Investment

The registration statement and prospectus are key documents which are jointly written, edited, and approved by your company, your attorneys, your accountants, the underwriter, and his counsel. The documents can briefly be described as the written description and disclosure to the SEC and the investing public of certain material and pertinent information regarding your company, its operations, products, market, financial condition, financial performance, management, history, etc. While a fairly common format is usually observed in their structure, these two documents invariably end up being written, rewritten, and edited time and time again. All the attorneys involved will quibble over such things as the style of writing, punctuation, word choice, and the like. To make matters worse, this behavior can continue after the documents have been set in type by the printer, requiring numerous typesetting revisions, more proof copies, and overtime at considerable cost. The amount of money which can be squandered in the process of preparing these documents is frightening, and most of it will come out of your pocket.

You probably cannot eliminate all the rewrites, but you can reduce their frequency and cost. One method is for you and your staff to prepare the first few drafts of the sections relating to the description of your business and its operations, using some of the prospectuses you have previously collected as models. Follow them closely, substituting, where appropriate, the factual data, information, and description of your company in your own words and style. Have these drafts prepared by a secretary using a word processor to make changes easily, quickly, and inexpensively.

Your attorneys should normally play the lead role in organizing, scheduling and managing the preparation of the registration statement and prospectus. You probably have no expertise in SEC requirements and should not attempt to practice law; however, you probably are a good manager and leader and should make use of those talents. You are the one paying the bills, and it is to your economic advantage to take the initiative and demonstrate your intent to have things done properly and quickly by all the participants. See if you can organize a disciplined effort to get most of the prospectus written in as brief a time as possible by organizing the following sessions about one week into the master timetable:

1. Have all the various professional participants (including the underwriter and his legal counsel) and your staff in your of-

fice at 9:00 A.M. on Monday morning. They should have been previously alerted that the objective is to write the entire prospectus over the next five days.

2. Distribute the first preliminary draft of the business description you and your staff have previously prepared. It will serve as a good starting point even if it ends up totally changed.

3. Divide the group into two or more teams, making certain that each team has at least one member of your staff who knows the company's business, products, industry, etc. For example, you and your chief financial officer should be on different teams. Assign each team specific portions of the prospectus to write.

4. Organize appropriate desk/office space for each team and have typists standing by to re-type and reproduce revisions as they are made.

5. Get the teams back together for a 2:00 P.M. working lunch (lasting no more than one hour) and have each team report on its progress and requirements. Each team should distribute copies of its draft sections for the others to review. After lunch have them go back to their respective office areas.

6. At 7:00 P.M., get the teams back together for a working dinner (lasting no more than two hours). At the conclusion of the dinner, collect whatever has to be re-typed and have typists available that night so that fresh drafts will be ready by the following morning's session, scheduled to begin at 9:00 A.M.

7. Start the Tuesday session by reviewing what has been accomplished and what still must be done. Again, provide desk space, typists, lunch, and dinner as you did on Monday. By Tuesday's dinner, some consensus should have been reached on a semifinal draft for many of the sections. Schedule the next session for Thursday at 9:00 A.M., thereby giving everyone a day to work on other matters while your attorneys pull together all the work that has been accomplished into one cohesive master draft.

8. Start the Thursday session by distributing the master draft to all participants. Spend the morning and lunch together going over the master draft, line by line. After lunch, have each team go to its area to work on the sections that require modification based on the morning discussion. At the 7:00 P.M. dinner, collect all the revisions and have your typists prepare a new master draft for Friday's session.

9. Start Friday's session at 9:00 A.M. by distributing the new master draft to all participants. Everyone will stay together today, reviewing every line of the draft. Changes, if any, will be worked out with everyone participating together, and agreement must be reached on a proposed revision before you move on to the next item to be changed. By the end of the Friday session (which might last until midnight), the group should have reached agreement on a final draft of the prospectus. Logos, artwork, print style, and paper stock should be reviewed and approved at this time.

10. At the conclusion of the Friday session, your attorneys should take responsibility for the following up on any unresolved items and typing up the final draft. While you can be sure of further changes to the final draft, they should be very minor.

By your organizing intensive working sessions and concentrating everyone's efforts on the prospectus, the document will be completed as quickly, economically, and professionally as possible.

14

SEC Review, "Blue Sky" Laws, and Final Negotiations

THE REGISTRATION STATEMENT IS FILED WITH THE SEC, AND WHILE waiting (approximately two to four weeks) for the SEC to perform its review and/or allow the offering to become "effective," copies of the preliminary prospectus, the *"red herring,"* are distributed to members of the underwriting syndicate and the investing public. Printed on its front cover in red ink must be a statement indicating that a registration statement has been filed, but has not become effective, and that the securities are not being sold, or offered for sale, nor are orders being solicited, prior to the effective date. The "red herring" does not indicate an offering price or the underwriter's compensation. While the underwriter is unable to make any sales during the *waiting period,* the "red herring" does, in reality, function as a selling tool and is distributed to determine the interest in the offering.

SEC Review of Your Documents

During the waiting period, the SEC is reviewing the registration statement to see if adequate and appropriate disclosures have been made. The depth and intensity of review can vary and is solely deter-mined by the SEC staff doing the review. The SEC almost always has questions and comments regarding the information (or lack of information) in the registration statement. They will communicate these to you either by phone or through a formal letter of comments called a *deficiency letter*. Usually, your attorneys, the underwriter's counsel, and other key participants have one or more conference calls with the SEC staff members to permit a discussion and understanding of the questions and comments raised. Depending upon how significant the questions and comments are, and the nature and complexity of the information or changes necessary to satisfy the SEC, the corrective action may vary. Some matters can be resolved by an explanatory letter to the SEC, others might require that amendments to the registration statement, while still others might require that the preliminary prospectus must be revised and recirculated as well. You usually have little choice in the matter; it is best to satisfy the SEC as quickly and as simply as possible. Any protracted negotiation or discussion can cost you valuable time in getting to market, as well as rapidly escalating attorney's fees.

State "Blue Sky" Laws

Although you will have filed a registration statement with the SEC, the company must still have its securities "qualified" in the states where the underwriter expects to sell the securities. The state laws that regulate this matter are referred to as *"blue sky laws."* The term "blue sky" goes back to a famous 1915 federal court case in which Justice McKenna referred to "speculative schemes which have no more substance than so many feet of blue sky."

Usually, the underwriter will want to have the offering qualified in those states that typically are active investment markets, either from a standpoint of the potential individual investor population or the number of investing institutions resident in the state. For example, underwriters will want to be qualified in New York, New Jersey, Massachusetts, Texas, California, Illinois, Connecticut, Pennsylvania, Delaware, and Florida. In addition, the offering should be qualified in the states in which the company has facilities, operations, major customers, or other activities that generate high public visibility and recognition.

Almost every state now has some form of "blue sky" law for the protection of its citizens. The federal statutes dealing with the registration, sale, and exchange of securities do not interfere with the operation of the state laws, and satisfaction of the federal requirements does not mean automatic approval of the IPO in all the states. Special forms, applications, and information requirements must be filed and approved.

While there is considerable uniformity in the securities laws among the states, there are still significant variations that require careful preparation to satisfy all the procedures, standards, and disclosure requirements of the individual jurisdictions. Some state securities commissions perform a detailed review of the registration statement and supporting data; others perform a cursory review at best, relying instead upon the review by the SEC.

Major areas of concern to those states that perform detailed reviews seem to center on "sweetheart" deals and non-arm's-length transactions with insiders regarding loans or "cheap stock" given in exchange for property or services. Shareholder voting rights, anti-takeover protection terms, and other provisions in the charter and bylaws of the company are also given close scrutiny.

A state can prohibit the sale of securities within its borders unless the company makes appropriate changes in the registration statement, disclosures, charter, bylaws, agreements with insiders, or other matters that the state finds unacceptable. Often, matters in dispute can be resolved through compromise and negotiation with the state's examiner. If the state represents a major market for the stock offering, the underwriter (and members of the marketing syndicate) will put pressure on the company to make the necessary changes, but the company can refuse (or might be unable) to make those changes and thus forgo registration within that state.

Usually, the underwriter's counsel will have the most experience in, and perform the necessary legal work for, the company regarding the "blue sky" registrations. Routine legal fees in connection with such services will run between $5,000 and $20,000 depending upon how many and which states are involved.

Final Negotiations with the Underwriter

Meanwhile, the underwriter and the syndicates (if any) organized to market the stock and take the underwriting risk will be distributing the preliminary prospectus and talking to potential investors. The managing underwriter usually keeps track of the orders and commitments, which is called "running the book" on the offering. All of this takes place before the final underwriting agreement is signed by the company and the managing underwriter. Although some of the commitments might not materialize at the last minute, a good underwriter knows quite well how the offering will actually go once it is "effective."

Usually, the day before the registration statement is to become effective, the company and the underwriter will negotiate the offering price for the shares. As you will recall, while there were earlier discussions and understandings on this subject, this is the time when the formal, final agreements are completed by your company and the underwriter. Depending on the current stock market conditions, the degree of the market's interest in your offering (as discerned by the underwriter and his marketing syndicate), and your own business judgment, the offering price and the underwriter's compensation will be finalized.

Your company has invested a great deal of time and money in the offering process so far, and there is the risk that, for a variety of reasons, the now-proposed offering price might be significantly below your expectations. You must be prepared, factually and emotionally, for some difficult decisions. Your choices are:

- accept the lower price and proceed with the offering,
- postpone the offering on a day-to-day basis until the market or the market's interest in your offering improves, or
- withdraw the offering for an indefinite period of time, knowing that much of the effort and money expended will have been wasted.

The potential for this problem lurks in the background from the first moment you decide to go public. You can and should prepare yourself and your organization for the decisions and consequences that could result if this comes to pass. Keep yourself abreast of the market and investor interest in your company; make a point to question the underwriter on that subject regularly—initially once a week and then, as you approach the final 10 days, on a daily basis. If the interest is weak or weakening, you want to know it early. Follow what is happening to the stock market in general and to the stock prices of public companies in the same business as yours or in associated businesses. Make certain that you maintain control of the financial condition of the company. Do not let the euphoria of the expected influx of funds from the offering cause financial extravagance and overcommitments. If you are faced with making a difficult decision on this problem, at the very least, you want some flexibility of action. A decision of this magnitude requires that you discuss the potential ramifications with all of your internal and external advisors. Don't react emotionally, fearfully, angrily, or hastily.

Assuming you reach agreement and the offering is to proceed, a carefully organized frenzy of document signing takes place at which all the final contracts between the company and the underwriter are completed. If the underwriter has organized a purchase syndicate to participate in the offering, there will also be agreements among the underwriters to be signed. All necessary amendments to the registration statement will be filed with the SEC, including the *pricing amendment,* which specifies the offering price and the underwriter's compensation. "Blue sky" registrations are completed and submitted to the various states.

As soon as formal clearance is received from the SEC and appropriate state authorities, the printer is given all final changes and/or pricing information and completes the printing of the final prospectus. The final prospectus is distributed to anyone interested in purchasing the stock and to anyone who purchases the stock at the offering.

15

The "Dog and Pony Show," the Closing, and What Comes After

AFTER THE REGISTRATION STATEMENT IS FILED AND WHILE THE SEC is performing its review, the underwriter and certain top executives of the company will probably go out on what is sometimes called the *"dog and pony show."* The underwriter might set up a series of meetings in a number of cities at which the company officials are introduced to other members of the underwriting syndicate, institutional investors, portfolio managers, security analysts, and others who might have an interest in the offering. Video teleconferencing facilities can also be an effective tool when the schedule does not permit in-person visits to distant cities. The "almost face-to-face" interaction provided by such facilities is an acceptable substitute when circumstances so dictate.

These meetings, often several per day, are important opportunities for the company to tell its story, explain its potential for growth, and generate a demand for its stock. While you will probably make a brief, prepared statement at the meetings, there is usually a far-ranging question-and-answer period during which you and your executives will have to respond on an ad-lib basis. Your answers and those of your staff are part of the selling process and present a golden opportunity to "sell the sizzle" about your company. Not all of the questions you get will make sense, and some of the people doing the questioning will not have read the preliminary prospectus or understood very much about your company or its business. Many of the people you will be speaking to, however, are the decision makers and those who influence the decision makers. They can make or break your offering.

Visual aids, including video tapes, charts, and product samples, can and should be used to supplement the presentations, if at all possible. Make certain, however, that the material used is of professional caliber, not boring, and integrated into a well-prepared "pitch."

Many companies making a stock offering are engaged in a "familiar" business, that is, one which is not particularly unique or exciting no matter how well it is doing financially. "Selling the familiar" can be difficult. To stimulate investor interest in this type of company, use carefully selected and prepared visual material rather than a long-winded verbal presentation.

The company must demonstrate that it has a promising future and is intelligently managed by an honest, capable team of qualified executives. No one can successfully bluff his way through these meetings, and to try to do so invites disaster. Every executive present must know what he is talking about and be able to think on his feet and express himself in a satisfactory manner. The way the executive team talks, dresses, and acts can have an enormous impact on the success of the underwriter's marketing efforts. If liquor is served at luncheon or dinner meetings, abstinence is a prudent policy for all the members of your team. Save the celebrations until after the offering is consumated.

Over-allotments and the "Short" Position

During the actual offering, the underwriters might offer for sale more shares than they are obligated to purchase under the terms of the underwriting agreement. This practice is generally called "*over-allotment.*" Since the underwriter is selling shares that he does not have, he has created a "*short*" position, or *short sale.* Experience has shown, however, that many buyers of the initial offering will sell their shares just a few days later. This is especially true if the stock price does not quickly run up above the offering price. When those sell orders reach the market, they can push the share price below the initial offering price. By having oversold initially, the underwriter can cover his "short" position by *stabilization*—purchasing the shares being sold by the early sellers and thereby helping support or stabilize the market price.

The "Green Shoe" Option

It is also quite normal for the underwriting agreement to give the underwriter a time-limited (usually 30-day) option to purchase additional shares from the company on the same terms, conditions, and price as the basic offering. This option is commonly referred to as a *"green shoe,"* and is usually limited to a maximum of an additional 10 percent of the number of shares in the basic offering. If the market price of the stock holds up and there are insufficient early sellers to enable the underwriter to cover his "short" position without forcing the market price up, he can exercise the "green shoe" option to cover his over-allotment activities.

The Closing Meeting: Getting the Proceeds

A successful offering will "close" approximately seven to ten days after it became "effective," and a *closing* meeting will be held. At this meeting (usually attended by the company and its attorneys, the underwriter and its counsel, the accountants, the registrar, and the transfer agent), various documents, stock certificates, funds, and acknowledgements are exchanged. The company receives a check for the net proceeds of the offering, and the underwriter receives the stock certificates. Because the amount of money to be received is usually substantial, the company should try to have the meeting conclude before noon and have earlier requested that its proceeds be received in a form that will permit their transfer as "immediately available collected funds" into the company's bank account. Instructions should be left with your bank to invest the funds, at least overnight, to earn interest in the company's behalf. If this is not done, it may take several days for the underwriter's check to clear, and several days' use of the money will be lost.

Avoiding Future Problems

Now that it is "public," your company and all of its key executives become subject to a variety of complex laws, rules, regulations, and expected behaviors. None of these should be a surprise, as they should have been discussed in depth by you, the officers and directors of the company, and the accountants and attorneys prior to making the decision to go public. It would be prudent to now have another top-level meeting to permit a review of the new requirements and restrictions. The company's attorneys must play the lead role in explaining and communicating the issues involved. Formal guidelines should be prepared and distributed to all parties, and appropriate internal records and procedures should be implemented to prevent the company or any of its officers and directors from committing any infractions of the securities laws.

Investor Relations After the Offering

Attracting and retaining the attention of the investment community is in the best interests of the company, as well as its stockholders. After their IPOs, many companies neglect to develop a complete investor relations program. This is a very shortsighted attitude and can adversely affect the company's stock price on an on-going basis, and its ability to raise additional capital in the future. A good relationship with the investment community requires an allocation of time and money by management. A financial public relations firm can be used to assist the company in developing and implementing a program, but it is no substitute for management's full participation and commitment. Regular meetings with stock analysts and investment advisors, at your company's facilities, New York, and other cities, are an important part of the program.

One senior executive (excluding yourself) should be designated as the primary contact for the investment community. The executive designated should be knowledgeable, articulate, and have your confidence. Usually the chief financial officer gets that assignment and should be able to handle much of the day-to-day contact. While you should be accessible to the investment community, you do not need to personally handle every situation.

The goodwill and respect that results from an effective financial relations program will support investor interest and the company's stock price through both good times and bad.

16

Printing Costs and Miscellaneous Expenses

IN ADDITION TO ACCOUNTING AND LEGAL COSTS, YOUR COMPANY WILL incur several other expenses that can add up to a significant amount of money.

Printing Costs

The printing bill for the registration statement, prospectus, and other forms involved in the typical offering can reach $100,000, and can be significantly higher if portions are printed in color (e.g., pictures of company products). Most cities have a few printers who are experienced *financial printers*. Such firms are specialists in the unique style, format, type size, and other requirements of the registration statement and prospectus. They usually have conference rooms for their clients, ample communications facilities, food service, administrative support staff, and round-the-clock typesetting operations to facilitate the last-minute revisions and changes which will invariably be made. The choice of printer should be made early, and they should be contacted and given your approximate timetable. If at all possible, select a qualified printer located in the same city as you and your outside professional staff. If anyone has to do extensive and expensive travel to the printers, it should be the underwriter and his team.

A rough estimate of the number of pages in each document and the number of copies of each document to be printed should be given to the printer to obtain a printing cost estimate. Ask the printer to separate the typesetting costs from the printing costs in his estimate. Because the printer will have no idea of how many changes will be reset in type or how much overtime will be needed, you can expect his estimate to run on the low side. Have your attorneys contact another local financial printer to validate the first quote.

After the final draft is set in type and a handful are run off by the printer on a special proof-press, last-minute corrections will be required. While these cannot totally be avoided, they can be minimized by coordinating the writing and re-writing efforts as previously outlined. Several thousand copies of a preliminary prospectus (the so-called "red herring") are printed and distributed by the underwriter as part of their marketing effort while awaiting SEC review of the proposed offering. As a result of its review of the documents, the SEC might require certain changes, clarifications, or additional data in the registration statement or prospectus.

When the SEC declares your registration effective, final details of the offering (per-share price, underwriter's compensation, aggregate offering value, etc.) are set in type and thousands of copies of the final prospectus are printed and sent to the underwriter and his syndicate for use as the selling document for the offering. The print run of the prospectus should be realistic. You do not want to be short and require an expensive re-run, but you also do not want to print tens of thousands extra. A moderate excess is the objective, as you will have other good uses for a few thousand leftovers.

When you receive the printer's bill, go over it carefully; if it deviates significantly from your expectations, review it in detail with the printer before paying. Make certain that the printer has given you a detailed analysis including a segregation of typesetting costs, revision costs, printing, and other costs.

Other Costs and Expenses

Now that your stock will be publicly traded, your company will have printed a large supply of blank stock certificates to be issued to the purchasers of your stock at the offering, and to provide replacements as the shares are traded in the aftermarket. The engraved plates necessary to print the certificates require a one-time investment of up to several thousand dollars, and the individual certificates can cost up to a dollar each, depending upon how fancy you want them.

Historically, stock certificates were usually prepared in two different formats. One standard format was in 100-share denominations; the other was for an unlimited number of shares. The majority of trades in a stock are made in even 100-share lots, and the preparation of a certificate form to represent a 100-share lot owned by a single stockholder was typical. But many transactions are for other than 100-share lots, and the use of the "unlimited" certificate format permits the issuance of certificates in any amount. Spaces are provided for insertion of the correct share amount in both numerals and words. Using the "unlimited" format exclusively is the most economical route for a company. Fewer certificates will be required and the entire process simplified.

The company will also engage the services of a *registrar* and a *transfer agent* (usually a bank or trust company) to manage and maintain the records relating to authorized shares, share ownership, transfers of shares, and the issuance of share certificates. These firms will also perform the mailing of annual reports, quarterly reports, dividend checks, and other communications to shareholders. The fees and costs associated with these services depend upon the number of shareholders, the trading activity in the stock, and how often material is sent to the shareholders. Typical costs for such services are approximately $4000 to $10,000 per year, depending on the volume of transactions and number of shareholder accounts.

Other expenses include filing fees paid to the SEC, to the NASD, and to the various states for the "blue sky" applications. The company might also have to pay a tax to its state of incorporation based on the amount of new capital it has obtained.

Who's Minding the Store?

During the time that the preparations, negotiations, and activities concerning the underwriting are taking place, you and your management staff must still pay appropriate attention to the company's routine business affairs. Allowing the organization to get distracted from its primary mission of getting sales orders, producing quality products, making shipments on time, etc., is potentially the most expensive and costly activity of all. You must *plan* and *prepare* your organization for the disruption that will probably occur in internal communications and the chain-of-command due to the time demands placed on key executives by the registration process.

17

Conclusion

THE MANAGEMENT OF A PUBLICLY OWNED COMPANY WILL BE SUBject to direct and indirect pressure from its shareholders and the investment community to maintain steady growth in sales and earnings. Although almost every representative of the investment community you encounter will assert that he (or she) is a "long-term" investor, the reality is that many of them will continue to hold or recommend your company's stock only so long as the company and the price of its stock continue to do well. Because your company is now issuing quarterly reports on its operating results, there is a real danger that strategic management decisions will be made on the basis of their impact on short-term profits and stock price, rather than for the long-range benefit of the company. Do not permit this to happen; continue to apply the same standards of judgment and planning that brought the company to its present level of success.

If there are problems or decisions which might adversely impact short-term results, don't lie about them or try to deceive the investment community. Make an honest effort to explain the situation and what you can and will be doing about it. The investment community hates to be surprised, especially on the negative side. By the same token, avoid making specific projections or forecasts regarding the future financial performance of the company. No matter how well you think you have explained the caveats or couched your phrases, what will be remembered are the specifics of what you have said. If you fail to deliver on your "promises," the repercussions can be enormous. The credibility of the company and its spokesmen are extremely important. If it is lost, many years might pass before you regain the confidence of the investment community and their interest in your stock.

By all means, encourage and welcome the interest of shareholders and representatives of the financial community. You and appropriate members of the management team should seek every opportunity to reinforce the positive aspects of the company's image. Securities analysts will want to visit with you and other management personnel to become familiar with the operations of the company. These analysts, usually part of the research departments of brokerage and investment firms, mutual fund and private money managers and other influencial segments of the investment community, are of significant importance in developing and sustaining investor interest in your stock. Seek out opportunities to make presentations at analysts' meetings and conferences. You should also investigate engaging the services of a financial public relations consultant to assist and guide you in your investor relations program.

Local, national, and trade media may wish to interview you and write articles about you and the company. This free publicity can be of great value to the company. Not only does it draw attention to the company's stock, but it gives the company's products or services free advertising. Two cautions however: you can never be certain what "angle" the interviewer or reporter will decide to take in the final article, and nothing is ever "off-the-record" once you have uttered it. In his or her search for an interesting article, the reporter might present matters in a negative light, or facts might accidentally turn out misstated or twisted. Before you agree to be interviewed, ask the reporter what the theme of the article will be, and request the privilege of discussing the article with the reporter before it is published to assist in avoiding any factual errors. You don't have the right to edit the work, but you do have the right to protect yourself.

In the euphoria of a successful offering, don't forget the contributions to its success made by middle management and the rank and file of your company. Animosity might develop between top management and the other employees because of the wealth now associated with public stock ownership. Certainly the employees will be proud of achieving "public" status, but see to it that their rewards are more tangible. Seek out ways for the employees to share or participate in the future growth of the company and its stock price. Institute as broad a stock option or stock purchase plan for employees as possible. Your objectives are to reward above-average performance, maintain loyalty, and keep morale at a high level.

A successful IPO represents the culmination of months or years of planning, preparation, and effort by many participants. It is a significant accomplishment for the company, and by the businessmen who have been providing leadership and guidance to the organization. The funds received by the company not only provide an opportunity to seek continued economic growth and success, but also represent a moral and legal responsibility to manage the affairs of the company diligently, intelligently, and in the best long-range interests of its hundreds or thousands of stockholders. If you and your entire organization are not prepared to honor those responsibilities, then do not go public.

Appendix

Appendix:

Prospectus
of the
Alliant Computer
Systems Corporation

Reproduced herein (with the permission of the company) is a copy of the prospectus issued by the Alliant Computer Systems Corporation, Littleton, Massachusetts, in connection with its successful offering of 1,750,000 shares of common stock at $15.00 per share on December 17, 1986.

Alliant Computer Systems Corporation designs, manufacturers and markets a family of compatible, high-performance computer systems used for computationally intense engineering and scientific applications. The company's systems are designed to meet the increasing demands for computing capability which exceeds the performance of existing superminicomputers, but at a cost significantly below that of supercomputers.

The company filed a Registration Statement on Form S-1, including amendments thereto, with the SEC. This was a firm commitment underwriting. The managing underwriters were Morgan Stanley & Co., Inc., and Hambrecht & Quist, Inc. A large number of prominent international, national, and regional investment banking firms and underwriters participated.

Excluding any exercise of a "green shoe" option of up to 250,000 shares granted to the underwriters to cover over-allotments, if any, the offering would have yielded the following:

Gross Proceeds: 1,750,000 shares @ $15.00 per share	=	$26,250,000
Deduct: Underwriting discounts and commissions based upon 1,750,000 shares @ $1.04 per share	=	1,820,000
Proceeds before expenses		24,430,000
Deduct: Estimated expenses to company, including legal, accounting, printing and miscellaneous costs	=	585,000
Estimated net proceeds		$23,845,000

Underwriting commissions and discounts were 6.93% of the offering price ($1.04 ÷ $15.00). Underwriting commissions and discounts plus expenses incurred by the company totaled $2,405,000 or 9.16% of the gross proceeds and 10.08% of the net proceeds to the company.

PROSPECTUS

1,750,000 Shares

ALLIANT
ComputerSystemsCorporation

COMMON STOCK

All of the shares of Common Stock offered hereby are being sold by the Company. Of such shares, 1,450,000 shares are being offered in the United States and Canada by the United States Underwriters, and 300,000 shares are being offered outside the United States and Canada by the International Underwriters. See "Underwriters." Prior to this offering, there has been no public market for the Common Stock of the Company. See "Underwriters" for a discussion of the factors considered in determining the offering price.

THE COMMON STOCK OFFERED HEREBY INVOLVES A HIGH DEGREE OF RISK. PROSPECTIVE INVESTORS SHOULD CAREFULLY CONSIDER THE MATTERS SET FORTH UNDER "RISK FACTORS."

THESE SECURITIES HAVE NOT BEEN APPROVED OR DISAPPROVED BY THE SECURITIES AND EXCHANGE COMMISSION NOR HAS THE COMMISSION PASSED UPON THE ACCURACY OR ADEQUACY OF THIS PROSPECTUS. ANY REPRESENTATION TO THE CONTRARY IS A CRIMINAL OFFENSE.

PRICE $15 A SHARE

	Price to Public	Underwriting Discounts and Commissions	Proceeds to Company(1)
Per Share............................	$15.00	$1.04	$13.96
Total(2)	$26,250,000	$1,820,000	$24,430,000

(1) Before deducting expenses, estimated at $585,000, payable by the Company.
(2) The Company has granted to the United States Underwriters an option, exercisable within 30 days of the date hereof, to purchase up to an aggregate of 250,000 additional shares at the price to public less underwriting discounts and commissions for the purpose of covering over-allotments, if any. If the United States Underwriters exercise such option in full, the total price to public, underwriting discounts and commissions and proceeds to Company will be $30,000,000, $2,080,000 and $27,920,000, respectively. See "Underwriters."

The shares are offered, subject to prior sale, when, as and if accepted by the Underwriters named herein and subject to approval of certain legal matters by Davis Polk & Wardwell, counsel for the Underwriters. It is expected that delivery of the certificates for the shares will be made on or about December 24, 1986 at the office of Morgan Stanley & Co. Incorporated, 55 Water Street, New York, New York, against payment therefor in New York funds.

MORGAN STANLEY & CO.
Incorporated

HAMBRECHT & QUIST
Incorporated

December 17, 1986

PROSPECTUS SUMMARY

The following summary is qualified in its entirety by the more detailed information and financial statements appearing elsewhere in this Prospectus.

THE COMPANY

Alliant Computer Systems Corporation designs, manufactures and markets a family of compatible, high-performance computer systems, the FX/Series™, used for computationally intense engineering and scientific applications. The Company's systems are designed to meet the increasing demands for computing capability which exceeds the performance of existing superminicomputers, but at a cost significantly below that of supercomputers. The Company's systems are entry-level supercomputers (or "mini-supercomputers"), which significantly enhance computational performance through the combination of parallel processing, multiprocessing and vector processing. These features are integrated with the Company's proprietary FX/Fortran™ compiler and operating system, enabling the FX/Series to run most standard Fortran programs in parallel with little or no reprogramming. The end-user list prices for the Company's systems range from approximately $100,000 to over $1,000,000. Typical applications for the Company's computer systems include computer-aided engineering and design, circuit and semiconductor simulation, signal processing, geophysical analysis, aerodynamic simulation, molecular modeling and mathematical algorithm development. The principal markets served by the Company are major industrial, research, engineering and financial companies; national research laboratories; the U.S. government and defense suppliers; and universities. The Company sold its first commercial unit in September 1985, and at October 31, 1986 had sold 54 systems to 29 customers.

THE OFFERING

Common Stock offered....................................	1,750,000 shares(1)
Common Stock to be outstanding after the offering	9,411,168 shares(1)
Use of proceeds	For general corporate purposes, primarily working capital.
Proposed NASDAQ symbol...............................	ALNT

SUMMARY FINANCIAL DATA

(In thousands, except per share amounts)

	Year Ended December 31,			Three Months Ended			
	1983	1984	1985	Dec. 31, 1985	March 31, 1986	June 30, 1986.	Sept. 30, 1986
Statements of Operations Data:							
Net sales....................................	—	—	$ 4,406	$ 4,114	$ 4,010	$ 5,923	$ 8,570
Income (loss) before extraordinary credit	$(2,464)	$(3,927)	(4,762)	256	249	372	687
Net income (loss)	(2,464)	(3,927)	(4,762)	256	467	697	1,288
Income (loss) per share:							
Before extraordinary credit	(.39)	(.50)	(.58)	.03	.03	.04	.08
Net income (loss)	(.39)	(.50)	(.58)	.03	.06	.08	.15
Shares used in per share calculations.............	6,355	7,909	8,169	8,178	8,430	8,431	8,433

	September 30, 1986	
	Actual	As Adjusted(1) (2)
Balance Sheet Data:		
Working capital...	$12,412	$36,257
Total assets..	23,321	47,166
Long-term obligations	—	—
Stockholders' equity..	17,551	41,396

(1) Assumes the United States Underwriters' over-allotment option is not exercised. See "Underwriters."

(2) Adjusted to reflect the sale by the Company of 1,750,000 shares offered hereby and the anticipated use of the proceeds.

Except as otherwise noted herein, information in this Prospectus assumes that the over-allotment option for 250,000 shares granted to the United States Underwriters is not exercised and reflects (i) the conversion upon the closing of this offering of all outstanding shares of Preferred Stock of the Company into an aggregate of 5,875,391 shares of Common Stock and (ii) the filing of the Company's Restated Certificate of Incorporation on the date of the sale of the shares offered hereby. See "Description of Capital Stock."

No person is authorized in connection with any offering made hereby to give any information or to make any representation not contained in this Prospectus and, if given or made, such information or representation must not be relied upon as having been authorized by the Company or by any Underwriter. This Prospectus does not constitute an offer to sell or the solicitation of an offer to buy any security other than the shares of Common Stock offered by this Prospectus, nor does it constitute an offer to sell or a solicitation of any offer to buy any of the securities offered hereby by any person in any jurisdiction in which it is unlawful for such person to make such offer or solicitation. Neither the delivery of this Prospectus nor any sale made hereunder shall under any circumstance create any implication that the information contained herein is correct as of any date subsequent to the date hereof.

No action has been or will be taken in any jurisdiction by the Company or any Underwriter that would permit a public offering of the Common Stock or possession or distribution of this Prospectus in any jurisdiction where action for that purpose is required, other than the United States. Persons into whose possession this Prospectus comes are required by the Company and the Underwriters to inform themselves about and to observe any restrictions as to the offering of the Common Stock and the distribution of this Prospectus.

Until March 18, 1987 (90 days after the commencement of the offering), all dealers effecting transactions in the Common Stock, whether or not participating in this distribution, may be required to deliver a Prospectus. This delivery requirement is in addition to the obligation of dealers to deliver a Prospectus when acting as Underwriters and with respect to their unsold allotments or subscriptions.

TABLE OF CONTENTS

The Company intends to furnish its stockholders with annual reports containing audited financial statements reported upon by independent public accountants, and quarterly reports containing unaudited financial information for the first three quarters of each fiscal year.

Alliant, Concentrix, FX/1, FX/8, FX/Series, FX/Fortran and the Company's logo are trademarks of Alliant Computer Systems Corporation. UNIX is a registered trademark of American Telephone and Telegraph Company. VAX is a registered trademark and VAX/VMS is a trademark of Digital Equipment Corporation. Ethernet is a registered trademark of Xerox Corporation. Domain is a registered trademark of Apollo Computer Inc. Sun Network File System is a trademark of Sun Microsystems, Inc.

THE COMPANY

Alliant Computer Systems Corporation designs, manufactures and markets the FX/Series, a family of compatible, high-performance computer systems for computationally intense engineering and scientific applications. The Company's systems are entry-level supercomputers (or "mini-supercomputers"), with end-user prices ranging from approximately $100,000 to over $1,000,000. The FX/Series provides significantly enhanced computational performance compared to existing superminicomputers through the combination of parallel processing, multiprocessing and vector processing. Until recently, vector processing was available only through special purpose add-on devices or on very expensive supercomputers such as those manufactured by Cray Research, Inc., which range in price from approximately $5 million to $20 million each. Typical applications for the Company's computer systems include computer-aided engineering and design, circuit and semiconductor simulation, signal processing, geophysical analysis, aerodynamic simulation, molecular modeling and mathematical algorithm development.

The FX/Series performance is achieved by combining several features that distinguish it from other computer systems:

- *Parallel processing.* The FX/Series allows up to eight computational processors to work on a single application simultaneously. Alliant believes that the FX/Series is the first commercially available computer system to run most standard Fortran programs in parallel with little or no reprogramming.

- *Multiprocessing.* Alliant computer systems can run multiple programs simultaneously on different processors, providing high system responsiveness and throughput required in interactive, multi-user environments.

- *Vector processing.* Each computational processor contains an integrated vector processing unit, which speeds execution of certain applications by allowing a single machine instruction to operate on multiple data elements.

Alliant's FX/Series consists of two computer systems. The FX/1™ contains a single 64-bit computational processor and the FX/8™ contains from one to eight 64-bit computational processors. Each computer in the FX/Series is UNIX®-based, executes the same system and application software and employs the same major electronic components. From the perspective of the user, FX/Series computers differ only in delivered performance and configurability.

The principal markets served by the Company are major industrial, research, engineering and financial companies; national research laboratories; the U.S. government and defense suppliers; and universities. Purchasers of Alliant's products include companies such as American Telephone and Telegraph Company ("AT&T"), Amoco Corporation, Hughes Aircraft Company, and United Technologies Corporation; national research laboratories such as Argonne National Laboratory and Sandia National Laboratories; U.S. government entities and defense suppliers such as the U.S. Army and The Boeing Company; and universities such as Massachusetts Institute of Technology, Stanford University and the University of Illinois. The Company markets its products in the United States and Canada through a direct sales and service force of 73 persons operating from 16 sales and service offices. Alliant sells its FX/Series primarily to end users and to a lesser extent to original equipment manufacturers. The Company sold its first commercial unit in September 1985, and at October 31, 1986 had sold 54 systems to 29 customers.

The Company was incorporated in the State of Delaware on May 17, 1982. The Company's executive offices are located at One Monarch Drive, Littleton, Massachusetts 01460, and its telephone number at that location is (617) 486-4950. As used herein, the terms "Alliant" and the "Company" refer to Alliant Computer Systems Corporation.

5

RISK FACTORS

In addition to the other information in this Prospectus, the following factors should be considered carefully in evaluating the Company and its business.

Short Operating History. The Company commenced business operations in May 1982 and was in the development stage through September 1985, during which period it incurred substantial losses. At September 30, 1986 the Company had an accumulated deficit of approximately $8.9 million. The Company sold its first commercial unit in September 1985. Although the Company has been profitable throughout 1986, there can be no assurance that its revenues will continue to grow or that it will continue to be profitable in the future. See "Selected Financial Data" and "Management's Discussion and Analysis of Financial Condition and Results of Operations." Moreover, the computer industry has been experiencing a slowdown which, if it continues, could adversely affect the Company.

Competition. Competition in the computer industry is intense. The Company competes with several companies which have significantly greater financial, marketing and operating resources. The Company competes primarily with Digital Equipment Corporation and, to a lesser extent, Floating Point Systems, Inc. Several other established companies, including International Business Machines Corporation, are expected to broaden their computer offerings to include competitive products. The Company also encounters significant competition from several relatively new companies that are offering or completing development of mini-supercomputers. The Company can give no assurance that it will be able to compete successfully in the future. See "Business — Competition."

Technological Changes. The computer industry is subject to rapid and significant technological changes and frequent introduction of new competitive products, often at substantial price/performance advantages. To respond to these expected changes, the Company will be required to continue substantial investments in research and development, periodically enhance its existing products and successfully introduce new competitive products, and maintain price/performance advantages in its selected markets. The Company can give no assurance that it will be able to respond adequately to expected technological changes in the market or that any of its new products will receive favorable market acceptance. See "Business — Product Development."

Market Development and Software Availability. The mini-supercomputer market is a new and developing market and, as such; may not materialize as expected. Sales of the Company's products have been primarily to universities, government-funded research laboratories and other institutions with experimental or research facilities. In order to sustain its sales growth the Company must achieve significant penetration of commercial markets. The availability of additional software for the Company's products, particularly third-party applications software, is an important element in successfully marketing its products for commercial applications. Certain of the Company's competitors currently offer more third-party applications programs than the Company. There can be no assurance that sufficient third-party software will be available for the Company's products on a timely basis or, if available, that the Company will be successful in penetrating commercial markets. See "Business — Competition." Moreover, since the Company's computer systems are primarily purchased for engineering and scientific applications, the market for its systems is likely to be adversely affected by reductions in capital or research and development spending programs, both commercial and governmental. Because the Company believes that the market for scientific computers is enhanced by increases in Federal spending, budget reductions or limits on budgetary increases, especially in research and development programs, could adversely affect the Company's business.

Dependence on Key Vendors. Certain parts and components used in the Company's products are available only from a single source. Although the Company maintains safety stocks of certain of these items, the inability to obtain single source parts and components of the quality and in the quantity required, or failure to develop alternative sources if and as required, would adversely affect the Company's business. The Company has no agreements with its sole source suppliers. See "Business — Manufacturing."

Customer Concentration and Quarterly Performance.   Because of the high average sales price of the Company's systems, the long sales cycle and the relatively few customers to date, one or a few customers could account for a substantial percentage of the Company's quarterly or annual net sales. In 1985 three customers accounted for 59%, 25% and 12% of the Company's net sales, while for the first nine months of 1986, two customers accounted for 21% and 12% of that period's net sales, respectively. The Company does not expect that these customers will necessarily continue to be major customers in the future. The Company's systems generally are shipped promptly after receipt of purchase orders, and therefore the Company does not expect to have any significant backlog. Also, a substantial portion of the Company's shipments typically has occurred in the last month of the quarter. As a result, revenues and income can fluctuate significantly from quarter to quarter, based on customer require-ments and the timing of orders and shipments. While the Company believes that these factors will be mitigated as it expands its customer base and unit volume, no assurance can be given that it will be successful in doing so.

Shares Eligible for Future Sale.   Upon completion of this offering, a substantial number of shares of Common Stock will be freely tradeable or will become eligible for sale in the open market beginning either on the date of this Prospectus or 90 days after the date of this Prospectus. The directors and officers of the Company and certain other stockholders have agreed not to sell 6,331,388 shares held by them within 150 days after the date of this Prospectus, without the consent of the Representatives of the Underwriters. Since there has been no established market for the Common Stock prior to this offering, no prediction can be made of the effect, if any, that market sales or availability of shares for sale will have on the market price. Nevertheless, sales of a substantial number of shares of Common Stock in the public market may have an adverse impact on the market price. See "Shares Eligible for Future Sale."

USE OF PROCEEDS

The net proceeds to be received by the Company from the sale of 1,750,000 shares of Common Stock are estimated to be $23,845,000 ($27,335,000 if the Underwriters' over-allotment option is exercised in full). The proceeds will be used primarily for working capital purposes, including financing increases in accounts receivable and inventory, and to a lesser extent for the purchase of additional capital equipment. Until the proceeds are so used, the Company intends to invest the net proceeds in short-term interest bearing securities. See "Management's Discussion and Analysis of Financial Condition and Results of Operations."

DIVIDEND POLICY

The Company has not paid any cash dividends on its Common Stock and does not anticipate paying any cash dividends in the foreseeable future.

CAPITALIZATION

The following table sets forth the capitalization of the Company at September 30, 1986, and as adjusted to reflect the sale of 1,750,000 shares of Common Stock offered hereby:

| | September 30, 1986 | |
| | Actual | As Adjusted |
	(In thousands)	
Long-term obligations(1)	$ —	$ —
Stockholders' equity(2)(3):		
Series Preferred Stock, $.01 par value; 7,500,000 shares authorized, no shares outstanding	—	—
Common Stock, $.01 par value; 25,000,000 shares authorized, 7,657,864 shares outstanding, 9,407,864 shares outstanding as adjusted	76	94
Additional paid-in capital	26,375	50,202
Accumulated deficit	(8,900)	(8,900)
Total stockholders' equity	17,551	41,396
Total capitalization	$17,551	$41,396

(1) See Notes 5 and 6 of Notes to Financial Statements. At September 30, 1986 the Company had $77,768 of short-term debt.

(2) Reflects the conversion immediately upon the closing of this offering of all outstanding shares of Preferred Stock of the Company into an aggregate of 5,875,391 shares of Common Stock. See Note 7 of Notes to Financial Statements.

(3) Does not include, at November 30, 1986, (a) 1,030,316 shares of Common Stock reserved for issuance upon exercise of outstanding options granted under the Company's 1984 Restricted Stock and Stock Option Plan (the "Restricted Plan"), (b) 19,107 shares of Common Stock subject to outstanding warrants, (c) 114,037 shares issuable upon exercise of options which may be granted in the future under the Restricted Plan or (d) 300,000 shares which may be issued under the Company's 1986 Employee Stock Purchase Plan. See "Management — Stock Option Plans" and Note 7 of Notes to Financial Statements.

DILUTION

The net tangible book value of the Company at September 30, 1986 was $2.29 per share of Common Stock after giving effect to the conversion of outstanding shares of the Company's Preferred Stock. Without taking into account any other changes in such net tangible book value after September 30, 1986, other than to give effect to the sale of 1,750,000 shares offered hereby (after deduction of underwriting discounts and commissions and offering expenses), the pro forma net tangible book value of the Company at September 30, 1986 would have been $4.40 per share, representing an immediate increase of $2.11 per share to existing stockholders and an immediate dilution of $10.60 per share to new investors in this offering. The following table illustrates this per share dilution:

Public offering price..		$15.00
Net tangible book value before the offering(1)................	$2.29	
Increase attributable to new investors........................	2.11	
Pro forma net tangible book value after the offering..............		4.40
Dilution to new investors(2)		$10.60

The following table sets forth at September 30, 1986 the number of shares acquired from the Company, the total consideration paid and the average price per share paid by existing stockholders and by new investors in this offering:

	Shares Purchased		Total Consideration		Average Price Per Share
	Number	Percent	Amount	Percent	
Existing stockholders...............	7,657,864	81%	$26,658,413	50%	$ 3.48
New investors.....................	1,750,000	19	26,250,000	50	15.00
Total	9,407,864	100%	$52,908,413	100%	

The above computations assume no exercise of outstanding stock options or warrants. At November 30, 1986 there were outstanding stock options to purchase an aggregate of 1,030,316 shares of Common Stock at exercise prices ranging from $.70 to $8.50 per share and at an average exercise price of $1.78 per share, and warrants to purchase 19,107 shares of Common Stock at a per share price of $.70 (6,000 shares) and $1.75 (13,107 shares). To the extent these options and warrants are exercised, and additional options are granted in the future, there will be further dilution to new investors. See "Management — Stock Option Plans."

(1) Net tangible book value per share is determined by dividing the number of outstanding shares of Common Stock into the tangible book value of the Company (tangible assets less total liabilities).

(2) Dilution is determined by subtracting pro forma net tangible book value per share after the offering from the amount of cash paid by a new investor for a share of Common Stock.

SELECTED FINANCIAL DATA

The statements of operations set forth below for the years ended December 31, 1983, 1984 and 1985 and the nine months ended September 30, 1986, and the balance sheet data at December 31, 1984 and 1985 and at September 30, 1986 are derived from, and are qualified by reference to, the Company's audited financial statements included elsewhere herein. The statement of operations data for the period from inception in May 1982 through December 31, 1982 and the balance sheet data at December 31, 1982 and 1983 are derived from audited financial statements not included in this Prospectus. The statement of operations for the nine months ended September 30, 1985 is derived from unaudited financial statements which, in the opinion of the Company, reflect all adjustments (consisting only of normal recurring adjustments) necessary for a fair presentation of such results. The operating results for the nine months ended September 30, 1986 are not necessarily indicative of results that may be expected for the full year. This data should be read in conjunction with the financial statements, related notes and other financial information included elsewhere in this Prospectus.

	Inception (May 17, 1982) to December 31, 1982	Year Ended December 31,			Nine Months Ended September 30,	
		1983	1984	1985	1985	1986
		(In thousands, except per share amounts)				
Statements of Operations:						
Net sales	—	—	—	$ 4,406	$ 293	$18,503
Cost of sales.....................	—	—	—	2,416	273	6,858
Gross profit	—	—	—	1,990	20	11,645
Operating expenses:						
Research and development......	$ 164	$ 2,476	$ 3,898	4,450	3,621	3,521
Selling, general and administrative........................	48	269	817	2,611	1,717	5,998
Income (loss) from operations	(212)	(2,745)	(4,715)	(5,071)	(5,318)	2,126
Interest income, net..............	14	281	788	309	298	495
Income (loss) before income taxes and extraordinary credit	(198)	(2,464)	(3,927)	(4,762)	(5,020)	2,621
Provision for income taxes	—	—	—	—	—	1,313
Income (loss) before extraordinary credit........................	(198)	(2,464)	(3,927)	(4,762)	(5,020)	1,308
Extraordinary credit — tax benefit of loss carryforward	—	—	—	—	—	1,144
Net income (loss)................	$(198)	$(2,464)	$(3,927)	$(4,762)	$(5,020)	$ 2,452
Income (loss) per share:						
Income (loss) before extraordinary credit	$(.07)	$(.39)	$(.50)	$(.58)	$(.61)	$.15
Extraordinary credit............	—	—	—	—	—	.14
Net income (loss).............	$(.07)	$(.39)	$(.50)	$(.58)	$(.61)	$.29
Weighted average number of common and common equivalent shares outstanding	2,918	6,355	7,909	8,169	8,166	8,431

	December 31,				September 30,	
	1982	1983	1984	1985	1985	1986
				(In thousands)		
Balance Sheet Data:						
Working capital	$4,690	$1,825	$ 774	$13,639	$2,554	$12,412
Total assets	4,802	3,233	9,252	16,858	5,157	23,321
Notes payable - current portion	—	221	287	169	214	78
Notes payable - less current portion	—	364	271	61	88	—
Stockholders' equity	4,732	2,295	8,270	15,001	3,256	17,551

MANAGEMENT'S DISCUSSION AND ANALYSIS
OF FINANCIAL CONDITION AND RESULTS OF OPERATIONS

Results of Operations

The Company was in the development stage from its inception in May 1982 through the quarter ended September 30, 1985. During this period, operations consisted principally of planning, design and development activities for the FX/Series. The development period ended with the first commercial shipment of an FX/Series system in September 1985. The Company first recognized significant revenues in the fourth quarter of 1985, and had incurred cumulative losses of $11.6 million from inception through September 30, 1985.

The following table contains selected unaudited financial data for each of the last five quarters. The Company believes that this information reflects all adjustments necessary for a fair presentation of information for the periods presented. These operating results, however, are not necessarily indicative of results for any future period.

	Three Months Ended				
	September 30, 1985	December 31, 1985	March 31, 1986	June 30, 1986	September 30, 1986
	(In thousands, except per share amounts)				
Net sales	$ 293	$4,114	$4,010	$5,923	$8,570
Cost of sales	149	2,144	1,699	2,194	2,965
Gross profit	144	1,970	2,311	3,729	5,605
Operating expenses:					
Research and development	1,657	829	825	1,069	1,627
Selling, general and administrative	963	894	1,210	2,088	2,700
Income (loss) from operations	(2,476)	247	276	572	1,278
Interest income, net	41	9	224	173	98
Income (loss) before income taxes and extraordinary credit	(2,435)	256	500	745	1,376
Provision for income taxes	—	—	251	373	689
Income (loss) before extraordinary credit	(2,435)	256	249	372	687
Extraordinary credit — tax benefit of loss carryforward	—	—	218	325	601
Net income (loss)	$(2,435)	$ 256	$ 467	$ 697	$1,288
Income (loss) per share:					
Income (loss) before extraordinary credit	$ (.30)	$ .03	$ .03	$ .04	$ .08
Extraordinary credit	—	—	.03	.04	.07
Net income (loss)	$ (.30)	$ .03	$ .06	$ .08	$ .15

The following table sets forth selected unaudited financial data for each of the last four quarters as a percentage of net sales.

	Three Months Ended			
	December 31, 1985	March 31, 1986	June 30, 1986	September 30, 1986
Net sales	100%	100%	100%	100%
Costs and expenses:				
Cost of sales	52	42	37	35
Research and development	20	21	18	19
Selling, general and administrative ...	22	30	35	31
Total	94	93	90	85
Income (loss) from operations	6	7	10	15
Interest income, net	–	6	3	1
Income (loss) before income taxes and extraordinary credit	6	13	13	16
Provision for income taxes	–	(6)	(6)	(8)
Income (loss) before extraordinary credit	6	7	7	8
Extraordinary credit — tax benefit of loss carryforward	–	5	5	7
Net income (loss)	6%	12%	12%	15%

Net sales in the first quarter of 1986 were 3% less than net sales in the fourth quarter of 1985. Net sales in the fourth quarter of 1985 included $1,687,000 of customer test systems shipped in earlier periods and recorded as sales in the fourth quarter when the customers purchased such systems. In the second and third quarters of 1986, net sales increased over the immediately preceding quarters by 48% and 45%, respectively, resulting from increased unit sales.

Cost of sales as a percentage of net sales decreased from 52% in the fourth quarter of 1985 to 35% in the third quarter of 1986, primarily resulting from declining costs attributable to the increased volume of materials purchased. The Company also benefited from declining prices for semiconductor components. However, as a result of the recently signed trade agreement between the United States and Japan, the prices of semiconductor devices have increased and, if such prices continue to rise, the Company's cost of sales may increase in the future.

Gross margins may be affected by customer mix and product configuration. Generally, the highest levels of gross profit and gross margins are derived from the direct sale of large systems to commercial end users.

Research and development expenditures decreased slightly in the nine months ended September 30, 1986 as compared to the nine months ended September 30, 1985, primarily as a result of the completion of the Company's initial product design cycle during the quarter ended September 30, 1985. Research and development spending since the third quarter of 1985 has been directed toward new products and product enhancements. In order to maintain its competitive position and to develop new and improved products, the Company intends to continue to devote substantial resources to research and development. Accordingly, the Company expects that research and development expenses will increase in absolute amount but may fluctuate as a percentage of net sales. See "Business — Product Development."

Selling, general and administrative costs have increased since December 31, 1985, primarily as a result of the significant increases in the number of sales personnel and the administrative organization needed to support the Company's growth. The number of sales and administrative employees grew from 23 at December 31, 1985 to 77 at September 30, 1986.

Interest income has decreased since the first quarter of 1986 due to the reduction in short-term cash investments which have been used to finance the Company's growth.

The provision for income taxes for the nine months ended September 30, 1986 was partially offset by an extraordinary credit attributable to the Company's utilization of net operating loss carryforwards. At December 31, 1985 the Company had approximately $11,352,000 of net operating loss carryforwards and approximately $969,000 of investment tax credit and research and development credit carryforwards available to reduce future Federal income taxes. Such carryforwards begin to expire in 1997 if not used. The Tax Reform Act of 1986 (including the repeal of the investment tax credit and the reduction in the research and development credit) is not expected to have a material impact on the Company's business or results of operations.

The Company typically delivers products to its customers as soon as practicable after receipt of a purchase order and does not maintain a significant backlog. Also, a substantial portion of the Company's shipments typically has occurred in the last month of the quarter. Therefore, net sales and income can fluctuate significantly from quarter to quarter, based on customer requirements and the timing of orders and shipments. While the Company believes that these factors will be mitigated as it expands its customer base and unit volume, no assurance can be given that it will be successful in doing so.

Inflation has not had a significant effect on the Company's operations.

Liquidity and Capital Resources

To date, the Company has relied principally on the proceeds of the private sale of preferred and common stock (aggregating approximately $26,000,000) and, to a lesser extent, borrowings to finance its operations. At September 30, 1986 the Company had approximately $5,100,000 of cash and cash equivalents and a bank credit facility for up to $4,000,000, which was subsequently increased to $10,000,000. Borrowings under this credit facility are collateralized by the Company's assets and limited by specified levels of eligible accounts receivable and inventories. At September 30, 1986 the Company had no outstanding borrowings under this agreement.

The Company believes that the proceeds from the sale of the Common Stock offered hereby, together with internally generated funds and existing sources of capital, will be sufficient to meet its cash requirements through at least the end of 1987. Thereafter additional equity or debt financing may be required.

BUSINESS

Background

Superminicomputers ("superminis") achieved broad acceptance for engineering and scientific computing since their introduction in the mid-1970's. Their appeal derived from their relatively affordable price, ease of use and high degree of user interactivity — benefits that were not economically available on the centralized mainframe computers of that period. However, superminis have been limited by a basic architecture designed to serve the diverse needs of both commercial and technical computing and, therefore, cannot easily deliver the level of performance increasingly required in certain computationally intense engineering and scientific applications.

Most computers, including superminis, are "scalar" processors; that is, instructions operate sequentially on single elements of data. However, scalar processors have been inadequate for many computationally intense technical applications where shortening time-to-solution is critical. Further improvements in the performance of scalar processors are, to a large degree, limited by the speed of the circuits from which they are constructed. Computationally intense technical applications that are normally run on scalar computers may benefit from the use of optimization features such as "vector" processing, which speeds execution of certain applications by allowing a single machine instruction to operate on multiple data elements (vectors or arrays). Until recently, vector processing was available only through special purpose add-on devices (such as array processors) or on very expensive supercomputers such as those manufactured by Cray Research, Inc., which range in price from approximately $5 million to $20 million each.

Many users either do not desire to purchase special purpose add-on devices or are unable or unwilling to pay the multi-million dollar price for a supercomputer. As a result, demand has developed for computer systems which bridge the price/performance gap between superminis and supercomputers. These computer systems — referred to as "mini-supercomputers" — meet many of the performance requirements of computationally intense technical applications, but at a cost significantly below that of supercomputers.

In recognition of this demand, Alliant developed its FX/Series of mini-supercomputers which combines several features that distinguish its products from other computer systems, including the following:

- *Parallel processing.* The FX/Series allows up to eight computational processors to work on a single application simultaneously. Alliant believes that the FX/Series is the first commercially available computer system to run most standard Fortran programs in parallel with little or no reprogramming.

- *Multiprocessing.* Alliant computer systems can run multiple programs simultaneously on different processors, providing high system responsiveness and throughput required in interactive, multi-user environments.

- *Vector processing.* Each computational processor contains an integrated vector processing unit, which speeds execution of certain applications by allowing a single machine instruction to operate on multiple data elements.

By combining these features, Alliant has developed a family of high performance computer systems that provides solutions to complex scientific problems with a level of performance that is not available with superminis. FX/Series systems have end-user list prices ranging from approximately $100,000 to over $1,000,000.

Markets, Applications and Customers

The principal markets served by the Company are major industrial, research, engineering and financial companies; national research laboratories; the U.S. government and defense suppliers; and universities. Within the commercial market, the Company has focused on communication, semiconductor, aerospace, petroleum, automotive/transportation, financial and chemical companies. Sales of the Company's products have been primarily to universities, government-funded research laboratories, and advanced research and development laboratories of major U.S. companies. The Company expects that future sales of its products will be more broadly distributed among its targeted markets.

At October 31, 1986 Alliant had sold 54 systems to 29 customers. The following table sets forth certain information relating to its customers at that date:

Customers*	Applications
Industrial, Research and Engineering Companies:	
AT&T Information Systems†	Traffic planning, Speech processing
AT&T Technology/Bell Labs†	Signal processing, Molecular modeling, VLSI design
Amoco Corporation	Drilling simulation
Bell Communications Research	Transmission line analysis
Pacific-Sierra Research Corporation	Timesharing
Sabbagh Associates, Inc.	Engineering consulting
United Technologies Corporation	Mechanical CAD
National Research Laboratories:	
Argonne National Laboratory	Algorithm development
EG&G Idaho, Inc.	Classified
National Research Council of Canada	Radio astronomy
Sandia National Laboratories	VLSI design
U.S. Government and Defense Suppliers:	
AT&T Military Systems	Classified
The Boeing Company	Flight simulation
COLSA, Inc.	Classified
Computer Sciences Corp.	Classified
Hughes Aircraft Company	Flight simulation
The Analytic Sciences Corporation†	Image processing
U.S. Army†	Classified
Universities:	
California Institute of Technology	Chemical research
Massachusetts Institute of Technology†	Aerodynamics, Chemical research, Mechanical engineering, Seismology
New York University	Algorithm development
Stanford University	Artificial intelligence
University of California, San Diego, Scripps Institution of Oceanography	Oceanographic research
University of Geneva, Geneva Observatory	Radio astronomy
University of Illinois†	Supercomputer research, Electrical CAD, Geology
University of Oklahoma	Reservoir modeling
University of Stockholm, Stockholm Observatory	Radio astronomy
University of Texas	Quantum chemistry
OEM and Joint Marketing:	
Apollo Computer Inc.†	**
Sun Microsystems, Inc.	**

* Does not include three systems purchased by a financial customer with which the Company has nondisclosure agreements.
** These systems are being used for joint marketing and development purposes. See "Sales and Distribution."
† Multiple systems.

In 1985 AT&T (including its subsidiaries), University of Illinois and Apollo Computer Inc. accounted for 59%, 25% and 12% of the Company's net sales, respectively. For the first nine months of 1986, AT&T (including its subsidiaries) and the U.S. Army accounted for 21%, and 12% of net sales, respectively. The Company does not expect that these customers will necessarily continue to be major customers in the future. Until the Company's sales volume increases significantly, certain customers may account for a large portion of annual and quarterly net sales.

Products

Alliant's FX/Series currently consists of two computer systems. The FX/8 contains from one to eight 64-bit computational processors and the FX/1 contains a single 64-bit computational processor. Each computational processor has its own vector facility. Each computer in the FX/Series is UNIX-based, executes the same system and application software and employs the same major electronic components. From the perspective of the user, FX/Series computers differ only in delivered performance and configurability.

FX/8. The FX/8 uses parallel processing to provide fast time-to-solution for complex problems while supporting interactive users. The FX/8 is field expandable from one to eight computational processors without any modification to system or user software. Compute speed is usually increased as processors are added; for certain applications the speed-up over a one-processor system approaches the number of processors added. The peak scalar performance of an eight-processor FX/8 is 39 million instructions per second ("MIPS") and its peak vector performance is 94 million floating point operations per second ("MFLOPS"). The FX/8 can be configured with up to 80 Mbytes of physical memory and up to 256 Kbytes of cache memory. A description of the FX/Series architecture is set forth below under "Product Technology — System Hardware."

The FX/8 differs from other parallel systems in several fundamental respects. First, each FX/8 computational processor ("CP") is a high performance general purpose computer with integrated vector processing. Second, it runs most standard Fortran programs in parallel with little or no reprogramming. Third, parallel processing control is based in dedicated hardware, a proprietary design innovation that substantially reduces the software inefficiencies encountered in other approaches to parallel processing.

A minimum configuration FX/8 that includes one CP has an end-user list price of approximately $270,000, while a system with eight CPs, depending on the configuration, has end-user list prices ranging from approximately $700,000 to over $1,000,000. The average FX/8 configuration sold to date has included three to four CPs.

FX/1. The FX/1 is a desk-high multi-processing system that can be dedicated to a single application, used as a multi-user departmental system or used as a computational server on a network of technical workstations or personal computers. The FX/1 is fully software compatible with and uses the same major electronic components as the FX/8. A minimum configuration FX/1 has an end-user list price of approximately $100,000.

Product Technology

The Company's FX/Series architecture is designed to provide fast parallel execution of a single application. Key to the design is a combination of proprietary hardware and software that allows subdivisions of a single program to run concurrently on up to eight processors, thereby substantially reducing time-to-solution for certain computationally intense applications.

System Hardware.

The Alliant architecture is based on two types of interconnected processors:

- The *computational processors* ("CPs") are proprietary processors developed by the Company which support the system's parallel processing capability. Up to eight CPs can execute portions of a single job in parallel, substantially reducing time-to-solution. Each CP is a general purpose microprogrammed pipelined computer with integrated vector processing. The peak scalar performance for each CP is 4.875 MIPS and its peak vector performance is 11.8 MFLOPS. Compute speed is usually increased as CPs are added; for certain applications, the speed-up over a one-processor system approaches the number of processors added.

- Up to twelve *interactive processors* ("IPs") execute interactive user jobs and other operating system activities, including input/output, simultaneously with each other and with the CPs, thereby freeing the CPs to concentrate on the computationally intense portions of the user applications. Each IP is based on the industry-standard Motorola 68000 series microprocessors.

All CPs and IPs in an FX/Series computer share a global memory. This enhances the parallel execution of a single application and allows jobs to migrate efficiently among the IPs and CPs, maximizing utilization of all processors. The cache and physical memory systems are designed to provide the bandwidth required to service up to eight CPs and twelve IPs.

The major components of the FX/Series are illustrated by the following diagram of its architecture.

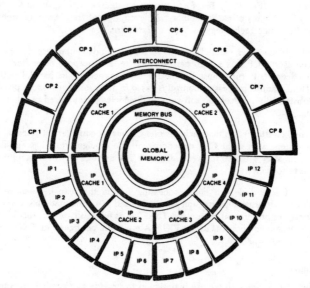

The FX/Series parallel architecture enables users to start with a system configured to their current needs, then readily upgrade to meet demand for higher performance. Installed systems can be expanded on-site with additional processors without reprogramming, recompiling or relinking of existing applications or system software. High reliability is achieved through the use of VLSI CMOS technology, with up to 256 Alliant-designed gate arrays in a single FX/8, that provides relatively low power consumption and operating temperature, and permits use of the Company's systems in normal supermini environments.

System Software

Alliant software is designed to allow users to exploit parallel processing across a wide range of scientific and engineering applications. Alliant believes that it is the only manufacturer to offer operating system and compiler software that allows standard Fortran applications programs written for conventional scalar computers to run in parallel with little or no reprogramming.

FX/Fortran Compiler. The Company's FX/Fortran is an ANSI-standard Fortran-77 that contains many of the extensions found in other popular Fortran compilers, such as Digital Equipment Corporation's VAX/VMS™ Fortran-77. Programs written for VAX/VMS Fortran-77 run on the FX/Series systems with little or no reprogramming. FX/Fortran automatically detects the potential for vector and parallel processing and generates instructions which implement the vector and parallel processing features of the hardware.

Alliant parallel processing allows FX/Fortran to optimize more of an application than is possible with a computer based on vector processing alone. Program constructs that execute in vector mode on vector computers are compiled by FX/Fortran to run in vector mode on Alliant systems. Alliant parallel processing also enables FX/Fortran to compile many code constructs for parallel execution on the FX/8 that do not lend themselves to vectorization. Because FX/Fortran optimizes more of the user's application, the FX/8 typically delivers a greater portion of rated peak performance than does a vector-only processor.

The Alliant FX/Fortran compiler automatically analyzes programs written in standard Fortran to identify loop constructs that can execute in parallel. Loops are compiled so that different iterations are processed in parallel on up to eight CPs. While data dependencies between iterations may inhibit vector execution on a vector-only processor, on an FX/8 they are automatically synchronized in dedicated hardware to minimize processing delays.

In addition to FX/Fortran, Alliant offers industry-standard C and Pascal language compilers. However, the vectorization and parallel processing features are not available in these languages without programmer intervention.

Concentrix Operating System. Alliant's Concentrix™ operating system is an enhanced version of Release 4.2 of the Fourth Berkeley Software Distribution ("4.2BSD"). Concentrix is a general purpose, multi-user operating system for scientific and engineering applications. Concentrix supports FX/Fortran, C, Pascal and the Alliant assembler.

Concentrix allows multiple resources to be applied to a single job and also permits multiple jobs to be efficiently scheduled. Concentrix can execute on any available CP or IP, but typically executes on an IP. This capability frees the CPs for execution of computationally intense programs, improves interactive response, supports multiple users and provides for expansion as the interactive load grows. Among the features of the Concentrix operating system are:

- *Multiprocessing.* In addition to parallel processing of a single program, Concentrix supports multiprocessing, which allows multiple user jobs to execute simultaneously on separate CPs and IPs. Multiprocessing provides high multi-user job throughput. Multiprocessing also allows Alliant users to exploit the parallelism that exists at the task level in many engineering and scientific programs. Using library features supplied by Alliant, programmers can develop "macro-tasking" applications that execute as coordinated, but independent, processes on multiple CPs.

- *Large Memory Support.* Up to 80 Mbytes of physical memory and two gigabytes of virtual program space are provided for very large problems.

- *Networking and Communications.* Concentrix allows Alliant systems to be tightly integrated into networks of engineering workstations, superminis and mainframes. Support is provided for industry and de facto standards for communications and networking, including Ethernet®, Apollo Domain®, TCP/IP with support for the Sun Network File System™, HASP and X.25.

18

Third-Party Applications Programs

The Company believes that a significant factor in a customer's selection among alternative computer systems is the availability of a broad range of third-party applications programs. The Company has arranged with a number of independent software developers to adapt their proprietary software programs to run on Alliant systems. At October 31, 1986 the Company had entered into agreements with 14 companies for 22 applications programs, of which 17 are currently available and five are being converted to run on Alliant systems. The Company believes that additional third-party agreements will be required for the long-term success of its business. See "Competition."

To stimulate and promote the adaptation of third-party software packages to run on Alliant computers, the Company has entered into joint marketing programs with third-party software companies and has agreed to support the conversion and marketing efforts by providing computer systems, technical assistance, financial incentives, minimum royalty payments, promotional literature and advertising. Under its existing third-party agreements, the Company is committed to pay a minimum of approximately $300,000 of future royalty payments. Alliant's third-party applications programs support mechanical computer-aided design, electrical computer-aided engineering, mathematical libraries, graphics and data base applications.

Sales and Distribution

Alliant sells its FX/Series primarily to end users and to a lesser extent to original equipment manufacturers ("OEMs"). At September 30, 1986 the Company had direct sales and customer support offices in or near 16 major cities throughout the United States. These offices are typically staffed with sales, applications support and customer service personnel. Field sales managers oversee both sales representatives and technical marketing support personnel. Post-sales support includes continuing consultation on software and applications, systems installation, maintenance and technical service. The Company plans to expand its sales and support staff and to add direct sales offices in 1987, primarily in those locations with high concentrations of technical industries and scientific applications. At September 30, 1986 the Company employed approximately 73 people in domestic marketing, sales and customer services.

The Company markets its products in Europe, Asia and Australia through Apollo Computer Inc. ("Apollo") pursuant to an agreement expiring in June 1988, subject to certain volume requirements. Apollo is obligated to use its best efforts to sell the Company's products, except in certain instances where there is significant competitive overlap with Apollo's own products, where logistics make support of the Company's products untenable or where the Company's products do not comply with local regulatory requirements. For the nine-month period ended September 30, 1986, sales to Apollo under this agreement amounted to approximately $235,000. Apollo also markets Alliant systems domestically in an OEM capacity under an agreement providing for the integration of Alliant systems into Apollo's product line. The Company also has an informal joint marketing arrangement with Sun Microsystems, Inc., which includes Alliant's support of Sun's Network File System. While the Company's primary marketing focus is on direct sales to large-account customers and to Federal government users or contractors, it also intends to expand its OEM activities.

Because the Company seeks to fill customer purchase orders as promptly as possible after receipt, the level of backlog at any particular date may not be a meaningful indicator of future revenues.

Service and Support

Alliant's customer service organization is responsible for installation, maintenance and repair, ongoing software consultation and comprehensive training for end users and OEMs.

The reliability of Alliant FX/Series systems is enhanced by the parallel system design. If a duplicate hardware module within a system fails, it is typically possible for Alliant service engineers, located at Alliant's customer service facility in Massachusetts, to remotely log into the affected system by telephone, run diagnostic software and identify and disconnect the failed component from the rest of the system. This remote diagnostic capability, together with the redundancy of certain hardware modules, often allows Alliant to restart the system without replacing the failed module. The Company also offers a cooperative service plan to customers in areas where nearby service is not available or who have in-house service capabilities. This program provides for replacement modules via an overnight delivery service.

The Company believes that reliable customer service and support is an important factor in customers' purchase decisions. Accordingly, the Company intends to add field support personnel, expand its parts inventory and increase the capabilities of its remote service center as the number of installed Alliant systems grows. The training, maintenance and support for products sold outside North America are provided by Apollo pursuant to its contractual responsibilities for international sales.

Alliant generally warrants parts and labor on its systems to end users for 90 days from installation. The Company also provides contractual maintenance and service for a fee after warranty expiration. Most of the Company's end-user customers have entered into maintenance contracts with the Company. These contracts normally are terminable by the customer at any time without penalty.

Manufacturing

The Company's manufacturing operations consist primarily of assembly, test and quality control of all parts, components and subassemblies and final system test. Subcontractors assemble printed circuit boards using electronic components which typically have been individually tested for prolonged periods. Assembled boards are then individually tested by the Company. Mechanical subassemblies are assembled in various stages until required for final assembly and systems test. During systems test, all elements of the system operating together are cycled through a series of acceptance programs to assure reliable operation in the field.

Although the Company generally uses standard parts and components for its products which are available from multiple vendors, it uses sole source suppliers for certain parts and components. The principal items available from only one source are adder and multiplier semiconductors manufactured by Weitek Corp.; gate arrays manufactured in Japan by Fujitsu Microelectronics, Inc.; microprocessors manufactured by Motorola Semiconductor, Inc.; and certain semiconductor parts manufactured by Fairchild Semiconductor, Inc. The Company is dependent upon the ability of these sole sources to deliver such items in accordance with the Company's specifications and delivery schedules. The failure of a supplier to deliver on schedule could delay or interrupt the Company's manufacture and delivery of products and thereby adversely affect the Company's revenues and profits. Although the Company endeavors to mitigate the potential adverse effect of supply interruptions by maintaining safety stocks of certain of these components or by developing alternative sources of supply for key components, the Company has no agreements with its sole source suppliers and there can be no assurance that such components will be readily available as and when needed.

The Company's manufacturing operations are located at its principal facility in Littleton, Massachusetts. Alliant believes that this facility is adequate for its manufacturing requirements through 1987. See "Facilities."

Product Development

The Company's product development efforts are focused on broadening the FX/Series by developing new computer systems and enhancing the hardware and software capabilities of its current products. The Company expects that many of the hardware and software enhancements currently under development will be introduced during 1987.

The hardware development programs include enhancements primarily designed to improve performance. These enhancements, which may be installed on existing systems through field upgrades, include larger memory subsystems, higher performance processors and input/output devices with higher bandwidth. In addition, the Company intends to continue implementing advanced VLSI semiconductor and packaging technology.

Among the system software development activities in which the Company is currently engaged are enhanced compilers, operating system enhancements, and additional tools, utilities, libraries, and communications software. While the Company develops most of its system software in-house, it supplements its developments through agreements with independent software developers and consultants for software design, implementation and program development.

During the years ended December 31, 1983, 1984 and 1985, the Company spent approximately $2,476,000, $3,898,000 and $4,450,000, respectively, on research and development activities. For the nine months ended September 30, 1986, it spent approximately $3,521,000 on these activities. Because the markets for the Company's products are characterized by rapid technological advances, Alliant intends to continue making significant investments in product development activities. During 1986, the Company adopted Statement of Financial Accounting Standard No. 86, "Accounting for the Costs of Computer Software to be Sold, Leased, or Otherwise Marketed." To date, no costs of internally developed software have been capitalized under this standard. The Company expects that compliance with this standard will not have a material effect on the Company's results of operations.

Competition

The computer industry is intensely competitive and subject to rapid technological advances, resulting in frequent new product introductions, increased capabilities and improvements in relative price/performance.

The Company has focused primarily on the scientific and engineering computing markets in which speed is critical to the solution of computationally intense problems. However, price, reliability and service, compatibility, the availability of third-party applications programs, networking, and user familiarity are also important competitive factors. Depending on the user's needs, this market can be served by a wide range of computer systems ranging from VAX superminis offered by Digital Equipment Corporation ("Digital") to supercomputers offered by Cray Research, Inc.

In its targeted market, the Company believes that Digital is its principal competitor. Digital is generally considered to be the leading manufacturer of superminis for scientific and engineering use, and most of the Company's customers and potential customers use Digital superminis. Digital is also believed to be developing a vectorization facility for its systems. The Company's products can be networked with Digital systems through industry standard protocols. See "System Software." The Company also competes with attached-processor and other systems offered by Floating Point Systems, Inc. In addition, certain other established computer companies, including International Business Machines Corporation, are offering or developing competitive products, or may elect to develop such products in the future. These companies have significantly greater financial, marketing and technical resources than the Company. In competing with such established vendors, the Company believes it must maintain a significant price/performance advantage.

The Company also encounters significant competition from several relatively new companies that are offering or completing development of mini-supercomputer products for the markets served by the Company.

The availability of a comprehensive library of third-party applications programs which run on the Company's systems is an important competitive factor. Certain of the Company's competitors currently offer more third-party applications programs. While the Company is seeking to expand its library of available third-party applications packages, no assurance can be given that it will be able to do so or that its library of programs will be as extensive as that of its competitors, in which event the Company's business could be adversely affected. See "Third-Party Applications Programs."

To respond to future competitive challenges, the Company plans to continue to offer products that are reliable, easy to use and capable of efficiently addressing the customers' desired uses at price/performance advantages over its competitors. The Company recognizes that this will require continued significant expenditures for product development and enhancements, including architectural improvements, new software capabilities, expansion of available applications software and effective, reliable customer service and support. See "Product Development." There can be no assurance that the Company will be successful in these efforts.

Employees

At September 30, 1986 the Company employed 193 full-time employees, of whom 57 were employed in research and development, 77 in sales, support and marketing, 45 in manufacturing and quality control and 14 in finance and administration. The Company's continued success will depend in large part on its ability to attract and retain trained and qualified personnel, who are in great demand throughout the industry. None of the Company's employees is represented by a labor union. Alliant believes that its employee relations are excellent.

Facilities

The Company's headquarters and its research and development and manufacturing facilities occupy approximately 102,000 square feet in a newly-constructed building located in Littleton, Massachusetts under a lease expiring in 1991, with two options to extend the term for five additional years each. The Company has the option to lease an additional facility to be constructed adjacent to its present facility. The Company also leases other facilities for sales and service offices in locations throughout the United States. The Company believes that its existing facilities are adequate to meet current requirements, and that suitable additional space will be available as needed to accommodate further physical expansion of corporate operations and for additional sales and service offices. The Company is also obligated through March 1988 to pay monthly rent of approximately $11,800 for its former facilities located in Acton, Massachusetts, together with certain maintenance fees and property taxes.

Patents and Licenses

The Company has four patent applications pending in the United States and corresponding patent applications pending in certain foreign countries. The patent applications relate primarily to the Company's product architecture. There can be no assurance that patents will be issued or that, once issued, the patents can be successfully defended. While patents may offer a measure of legal protection, the Company believes that they are less significant to the success of the Company than such factors as the innovative skills, technical expertise and management ability of its personnel.

The Company has entered into nonexclusive perpetual licenses with AT&T for the UNIX operating system and with the Regents of the University of California for 4.2BSD. Under each of these licenses the Company may grant sublicenses to its customers. The Company also has a perpetual license for certain compiler software from Pacific-Sierra Research Corporation. Under the foregoing licenses, the Company is obligated to pay royalties based upon system sales.

MANAGEMENT

Executive Officers and Directors

The executive officers and directors of the Company are as follows:

Name	Age	Position
Ronald H. Gruner	39	President, Chief Executive Officer and Director
Richard A. Cambria	48	Vice President, Human Resources
R. Stephen Cheheyl	41	Vice President, Finance and Administration
John P. Clary	49	Vice President, Manufacturing
Barry J. Fidelman	46	Vice President, International Sales
Richard T. McAndrew	40	Vice President, Hardware Product Development
I. David McDonald	43	Vice President, North American Sales
David L. Micciche	44	Vice President, Marketing, Sales and Customer Services
Craig J. Mundie(1)	37	Vice President, Software Product Development, Treasurer and Director
Carl D. Carman(1)(2)	50	Director
Thomas J. Perkins(2)	54	Director
Henry S. Smith(2)	43	Director

(1) Member of Compensation Committee

(2) Member of Audit Committee

Mr. Gruner, a founder of the Company, has been President, Chief Executive Officer and a director of the Company since May 1982. He previously was employed by Data General Corporation from 1969 to 1982, most recently as Director of Systems Development.

Mr. Cambria has been Vice President, Human Resources of the Company since July 1986. He previously was employed by GenRad, Inc. from 1973 to 1986, most recently as Vice President, Human Resources.

Mr. Cheheyl has been Vice President, Finance and Administration of the Company since August 1985. He previously was employed from 1983 to 1985 by The Saddlebrook Corporation, a software development firm, as Senior Vice President of Finance and Administration. From 1978 to 1983, Mr. Cheheyl was employed by Applicon Incorporated, principally as Vice President, Finance and Treasurer.

Mr. Clary has been Vice President, Manufacturing of the Company since January 1986 and from September 1983 through January 1986 served as Corporate Director of Manufacturing. He previously was employed by Data General Corporation from 1978 to 1983, most recently as plant manager for that company's Portsmouth, New Hampshire facility.

Mr. Fidelman has been Vice President, International Sales of the Company since January 1986. He previously was employed by Apollo Computer Inc. from 1981 to 1985, principally as Vice President, Worldwide Sales, Marketing and Services.

Mr. McAndrew, a founder of the Company, has been Vice President, Hardware Product Development of the Company since July 1982. He previously was employed by Computervision Corp. from 1976 to 1982, most recently as Vice President of Systems Hardware Products.

Mr. McDonald has been Vice President, North American Sales of the Company since January 1986. He previously was employed by Floating Point Systems, Inc. from 1981 to 1985, most recently as Regional Manager for the Eastern Region and Canada.

Mr. Micciche has been Vice President, Marketing, Sales and Customer Services of the Company since September 1983. He previously was employed by Digital Equipment Corporation from 1967 to 1983, most recently as Director of Marketing for the Office and Systems Group.

Mr. Mundie, a founder of the Company, has been Vice President, Software Product Development, Treasurer and a director of the Company since May 1982. He previously was employed by Data General Corporation from 1970 to 1982, most recently as director of its Advanced Development Laboratory in North Carolina.

Mr. Carman has been a director of the Company since May 1982. Since October 1983, he has been a General Partner of Masters Associates, a venture capital management firm which is the general partner of the Masters Fund, a venture capital investment fund. From October 1979 to October 1983, Mr. Carman was employed by NBI Inc., most recently as Executive Vice President. Mr. Carman is also a director of Cadnetix Corporation and MAPIT Corporation.

Mr. Perkins has been a director of the Company since December 1982. He has been a general partner of the General Partner of: Kleiner, Perkins, Caufield & Byers; Kleiner, Perkins, Caufield & Byers II; Kleiner, Perkins, Caufield & Byers III; and Kleiner, Perkins, Caufield & Byers IV, venture capital partnerships, since 1978, 1980, 1982 and 1986, respectively. Mr. Perkins is Chairman of the Board of Directors of Genentech, Inc., Tandem Computers Incorporated and Acuson Corporation and is a director of LSI Logic Corporation. For information relating to Mr. Perkins's relationship to one of the Representatives of the Underwriters, see "Underwriters."

Mr. Smith has been a director of the Company since December 1982. He has been a General Partner of Venrock Associates, a venture capital partnership, since June 1974.

Executive Compensation

The following table sets forth all cash compensation paid by the Company during the fiscal year ended December 31, 1985 to each of its executive officers whose total cash compensation exceeded $60,000, and to all executive officers as a group:

Name of Individual or Number of Persons in Group	Capacities in Which Served	Cash Compensation(1)
Ronald H. Gruner	President, Chief Executive Officer	$ 67,016
John P. Clary	Corporate Director of Manufacturing	67,167
Richard T. McAndrew	Vice President, Hardware Product Development	74,374
David L. Micciche	Vice President, Marketing, Sales and Customer Services	85,143
Craig J. Mundie	Vice President, Software Product Development and Treasurer	74,374
All executive officers as a group (six persons including the above)		$398,843

(1) Effective July 1986 the annual base salary for each of the Company's executive officers was fixed at $85,000 per annum, except for Mr. McDonald, whose annual base salary is $75,000. Each of the Company's executive officers, except Mr. Fidelman, participates in the Company's 1986 Executive Compensation Plan, which provides for the grant of quarterly bonuses based on the achievement of specified Company profit objectives in the preceding quarter. For the nine months ended September 30, 1986, each participating executive has earned a bonus of $7,239.

116

Directors of the Company currently receive no compensation for their services to the Company in such capacity, but are expected to receive directors fees commencing in 1987.

Stock Option Plans

1984 Restricted Stock and Stock Option Plan.

The Company has reserved an aggregate of 1,300,000 shares of Common Stock for issuance under its 1984 Restricted Stock and Stock Option Plan (the "Restricted Plan"), including 155,647 shares which have been issued pursuant to restricted stock awards and/or upon the exercise of options granted through November 30, 1986. The Restricted Plan is administered by the Board of Directors.

The Restricted Plan provides for the grant of incentive stock options (intended to qualify under Section 422A of the Internal Revenue Code of 1954, as amended (the "Code")), non-statutory stock options and restricted stock awards. All officers and key employees of the Company are eligible to receive incentive stock options, non-statutory stock options and restricted stock awards. Consultants, advisers, and outside directors of the Company are only eligible to receive non-statutory stock options and restricted stock awards. Persons owning 10% or more of the Company's Common Stock are only eligible to receive incentive stock options having a duration which cannot exceed five years and an exercise price which cannot be less than 110% of fair market value.

Stock Options. The Board of Directors selects the optionees and determines (i) the number of shares subject to each option, (ii) the dates the options become exercisable, (iii) the exercise price, which cannot be less than 90% of the fair market value for non-statutory options and less than 100% of the fair market value for incentive stock options and (iv) the duration of the option, which cannot exceed ten years. Payment of the option exercise price may be made in cash, shares of Common Stock or a combination of both. Options are not transferable except by will or the laws of descent and distribution and are exercisable during the lifetime of the optionee only while he or she is in the employ of or, if a consultant or adviser, is serving as a consultant or adviser to, the Company or within three months after termination of employment or consultancy except for discharge for cause (as defined). If termination is due to death, the option is exercisable for a one year period after death. If termination is due to disability, the option is exercisable for a six month period after termination. Generally, options may be exercised in full six months after the date of the grant, but the shares issued upon exercise of the options are subject to a right of repurchase by the Company at the original exercise price in the event of the termination of the option holder's employment or consultancy before specified periods. Generally, the shares vest and the repurchase right terminates as to 20% of the shares annually for five years from the date of the option grant.

Mr. Clary has received an incentive stock option to purchase 25,000 shares of Common Stock at an exercise price of $1.25 per share. None of Messrs. Gruner, McAndrew, Micciche or Mundie has been granted stock options under the Restricted Plan. All executive officers as a group have received incentive stock options to purchase an aggregate of 240,000 shares of Common Stock at an average exercise price of $.99 per share, and as a group have exercised options for an aggregate of 48,000 shares of Common Stock and realized an aggregate net value of $30,000 upon such exercise. In November 1986 the Company granted a stock option to purchase an aggregate of 57,000 shares of Common Stock, at an exercise price of $7.65 per share, to a firm providing technical consulting services to the Company. At November 30, 1986 options to purchase 1,167,163 shares had been granted under the Restricted Plan at an average exercise price of $1.37 per share, of which options for 136,847 shares had been exercised.

Restricted Stock Awards. Restricted stock awards entitle the recipient to purchase Common Stock from the Company under terms which provide for vesting over a specified number of years (usually five) and a right of repurchase of unvested stock when the recipient's relationship with the Company terminates. The Board of Directors selects the recipients of restricted stock awards and (i) determines the number of shares of Common Stock to be issued and sold to the recipient, (ii) the price of the stock, which can be less than the fair market value, but not less than the par value, of the Common Stock, and (iii) the vesting schedule for such shares. The recipient may not sell, transfer or otherwise dispose of such stock until it vests. Upon termination of the recipient's employment or consulting arrangement, the Company will be entitled to repurchase those shares which are not vested on the termination date at a price equal to their original purchase price. The repurchase right generally terminates as to 20% of the shares annually for five years from the date of the award.

In May 1985 and May 1986 each employee (other than executive officers) was granted an anniversary award of 100 shares of Common Stock under the Restricted Plan. These awards, aggregating 18,800 shares, were issued in consideration of past services and without any right of repurchase in favor of the Company. No other restricted stock awards have been made under the Restricted Plan to any directors, officers or employees of the Company. However, prior to the adoption of the Restricted Plan, 1,626,500 shares of Common Stock were issued to officers and employees, at a purchase price of $.05 per share, under restrictive terms similar to those contained in the Restricted Plan. Of these shares, 12,000 shares were subsequently repurchased by the Company, 1,093,000 are vested or will have vested as of December 15, 1986, and the remaining 521,500 shares will vest on various dates through March 5, 1989.

1986 Employee Stock Purchase Plan.

The Company's 1986 Employee Stock Purchase Plan (the "Purchase Plan") authorizes the grant of rights to purchase a maximum of 300,000 shares (subject to adjustment for stock splits and similar capital changes) of Common Stock to eligible employees in six semi-annual offerings. The Purchase Plan, which is intended to qualify under Section 423 of the Code, is to be administered by the Board of Directors or a committee of the Board of Directors. Each employee of the Company or of a subsidiary of the Company having at least thirty days of continuous service on the date of grant of a right will be eligible to participate in the Purchase Plan. However, any employee who immediately after the grant of a right is determined under the provisions of the Code to own 5% or more of the Common Stock would not be eligible to participate.

Rights will be granted twice yearly, on or about February 1 and August 1, and will be exercisable on or about the succeeding July 31 or January 31. Participating employees may elect to have from 1% to 10% of compensation (as defined) withheld for payment of the purchase price of the shares. During each offering, the maximum number of shares which may be purchased by a participating employee is determined on the first day of the offering period under a formula whereby 85% of the market value of a share of Common Stock on such date is divided into the applicable percentage of such participant's compensation (semi-annualized). The purchase price for shares will be the lower of 85% of the fair market value of the stock at the beginning or at the end of each semi-annual offering period. The Company expects that the first offering under the Purchase Plan will commence on or about February 1, 1987 and that the last offering will terminate on or about January 31, 1990.

CERTAIN TRANSACTIONS

In May and July 1982 an aggregate of 1,050,000 shares of Common Stock were purchased by Messrs. Gruner, McAndrew and Mundie, the three founders of the Company. Of the foregoing amount, Mr. Gruner acquired 400,000 shares, Mr. Mundie 350,000 shares and Mr. McAndrew 300,000 shares. All of these shares were acquired for cash, at a price of $.05 per share. Messrs. Gruner, McAndrew and Mundie may be considered "promoters" of the Company under the rules promulgated pursuant to the Securities Act of 1933, as amended. In September 1983 Messrs. Clary and Micciche acquired for cash, at a price of $.05 per share, 75,000 and 150,000 shares of Common Stock, respectively. In July 1986 Mr. Cheheyl purchased 40,000 shares of Common Stock pursuant to the exercise of an incentive stock option, at an exercise price of $.70 per share. In September 1986 Mr. Fidelman purchased 8,000 shares of Common Stock pursuant to the exercise of an incentive stock option, at an exercise price of $1.00 per share.

In private placement transactions pursuant to separate purchase agreements, the Company sold an aggregate of 5,875,391 shares of Preferred Stock issued in four separate series. Each share of Preferred

Stock is convertible into one share of Common Stock, and the Preferred Stock will be converted into an aggregate of 5,875,391 shares of Common Stock upon the closing of this offering (conditioned upon a sale price per share of Common Stock to the public of at least $12.50). In May 1982 the Company sold 500,000 shares of Series A Preferred Stock at a price of $.22 per share. In December 1982 the Company sold 2,742,857 shares of Series B Preferred Stock at a price of $1.75 per share. In March 1984 the Company sold 1,480,526 shares of Series C Preferred Stock at a price of $6.75 per share. In December 1985 the Company sold 1,152,008 shares of Series D Preferred Stock at a price of $10.00 per share.

As part of the financings described above, Kleiner, Perkins, Caufield & Byers III, a private investment firm of which Mr. Perkins, a director of the Company, is a General Partner, purchased 714,286 shares of Series B Preferred Stock, 444,444 shares of Series C Preferred Stock and 100,000 shares of Series D Preferred Stock. Venture capital funds managed by Hambrecht & Quist Venture Partners, of which David P. Best, a former director of the Company, was a General Partner, purchased an aggregate of 710,858 shares of Series B Preferred Stock, 444,444 shares of Series C Preferred Stock and 550,000 shares of Series D Preferred Stock. Hambrecht & Quist Venture Partners is associated with Hambrecht & Quist Group, the parent company of Hambrecht & Quist Incorporated, one of the two Representatives of the Underwriters of this offering. See "Underwriters." Venrock Associates, of which Mr. Smith, a director of the Company, is a General Partner, purchased 428,571 shares of Series B Preferred Stock, 148,148 shares of Series C Preferred Stock and 50,000 shares of Series D Preferred Stock. In addition, Mr. Smith individually purchased 28,571 shares of Series B Preferred Stock and 7,408 shares of Series C Preferred Stock. Mr. Carman, a director of the Company, purchased 250,000 shares of Series A Preferred Stock, 28,571 shares of Series B Preferred Stock and 3,704 shares of Series C Preferred Stock. Mr. Cheheyl, an officer of the Company, purchased 1,000 shares of Series D Preferred Stock.

The Company believes the shares issued in the above-referenced stock transactions were sold at their then fair market value and on terms no less favorable to the Company than could have been obtained from an unaffiliated third party.

The Board of Directors has voted that all transactions in the future between the Company and its principal officers, directors and affiliates will be approved by a majority of the disinterested members of the Board of Directors and will be on terms no less favorable than could be obtained from unrelated third parties.

PRINCIPAL STOCKHOLDERS

The following table sets forth certain information regarding the beneficial ownership of the Company's Common Stock at September 30, 1986 and as adjusted to reflect the sale of 1,750,000 shares of Common Stock offered hereby by (i) each person who is known by the Company to own beneficially more than five percent of the outstanding shares of the Company's Common Stock, (ii) each of the Company's directors, and (iii) all directors and officers of the Company as a group.

Names and Addresses	Number of Shares Beneficially Owned(1)	Percentage of Common Stock(1)	
		Before Offering	After Offering
Venture capital funds managed by Hambrecht & Quist Venture Partners(2) .... One Post Street San Francisco, CA 94121	1,705,302	22.27%	18.13%
Kleiner, Perkins, Caufield & Byers III .... Four Embarcadero Center Suite 3520 San Francisco, CA 94111	1,258,730	16.44	13.38

Names and Addresses	Number of Shares Beneficially Owned(1)	Percentage of Common Stock(1)	
		Before Offering	After Offering
Venrock Associates(3) .... 30 Rockefeller Plaza New York, NY 10112	626,719	8.18	6.66
Ronald H. Gruner	400,000	5.22	4.25
Craig J. Mundie	350,000	4.57	3.72
Carl D. Carman(4)	242,275	3.16	2.58
Thomas J. Perkins(5)	1,258,730	16.44	13.38
Henry S. Smith(6).....................................	662,698	8.65	7.04
All directors and officers as a group (13 persons)(7)	3,708,274	47.24	39.42

(1) Each stockholder possesses sole voting and investment power with respect to the shares listed opposite his or her name, except as otherwise indicated. Shares issuable to each five percent holder, director or officer under outstanding stock options are considered outstanding for the purpose of calculating the percentage of Common Stock owned by such person but not for the purpose of calculating the percentage of Common Stock owned by any other person.

(2) Includes shares held by funds managed by Hambrecht & Quist Venture Partners. Hambrecht & Quist Venture Partners is associated with Hambrecht & Quist Group, the parent company of Hambrecht & Quist Incorporated, one of the Representatives of the Underwriters of this offering.

(3) Does not include 35,979 shares held by Henry S. Smith, a General Partner of Venrock Associates and a director of the Company.

(4) Includes 25,000 shares held by Mr. Carman's wife.

(5) Includes 1,258,730 shares held by Kleiner, Perkins, Caufield & Byers III. Mr. Perkins may be deemed to beneficially own these shares because he is a General Partner of the General Partner of Kleiner, Perkins, Caufield & Byers III.

(6) Includes 626,719 shares held by Venrock Associates. Mr. Smith may be deemed to beneficially own these shares because he is is a general partner of Venrock Associates.

(7) Includes a total of 192,000 shares which officers of the Company have the right to acquire under outstanding stock options exercisable within 60 days after December 15, 1986. Also includes an aggregate of 1,885,449 shares held by Kleiner, Perkins, Caufield & Byers III and Venrock Associates. See Notes (5) and (6) above.

DESCRIPTION OF CAPITAL STOCK

After giving effect to the sale of the shares offered hereby and the filing of the Restated Certificate of Incorporation described below, the authorized capital stock of the Company will consist of 25,000,000 shares of Common Stock, par value $.01 per share, and 7,500,000 shares of Series Preferred Stock, par value $.01 per share.

Common Stock

The holders of Common Stock are entitled to one vote per share for each share held of record on all matters submitted to a vote of stockholders and are entitled to receive ratably such dividends as may be declared by the Board of Directors out of funds legally available therefor. In the event of a liquidation, dissolution or winding up of the Company, holders of Common Stock have the right to a ratable portion of assets remaining after payment of liabilities and liquidation preferences of any outstanding shares of Series Preferred Stock. The holders of Common Stock have no preemptive rights, cumulative voting rights, or rights to convert their Common Stock into any other securities and are not subject to future calls or assessments by the Company. All outstanding shares of Common Stock are, and the shares offered hereby by the Company upon issuance and sale will be, fully paid and nonassessable.

At November 30, 1986 (after giving effect to the conversion of the outstanding Preferred Stock), there were 7,656,948 shares of Common Stock outstanding, held of record by approximately 220 stockholders. There will be 9,406,948 shares of Common Stock outstanding (assuming the Underwriters' over-allotment option is not exercised) after giving effect to the sale of the shares of Common Stock offered hereby.

Preferred Stock

At November 30, 1986 an aggregate of 5,875,391 shares of Preferred Stock was outstanding. Upon the closing of this offering at a public offering price of at least $12.50 per share, each outstanding share of Series A, Series B, Series C and Series D Preferred Stock will be automatically converted into one share of Common Stock. The Preferred Stock so converted will be cancelled and may not thereafter be reissued. Effective upon the filing of a Restated Certificate of Incorporation, to be filed immediately following the consummation of the sale of the shares offered hereby, the Company will have a new authorized class of Series Preferred Stock consisting of 7,500,000 shares. Such Series Preferred Stock may be issued in series with such rights, preferences and privileges as the Board of Directors may determine. The issuance of Series Preferred Stock may have the effect of delaying, deferring or preventing a change in control of the Company whether or not beneficial to public stockholders and without further action by such stockholders. The issuance of Series Preferred Stock with voting and conversion rights may adversely affect the voting power of the holders of Common Stock, including the loss of voting control to others. The Company has no present plans to issue any additional Series Preferred Stock. See Note 7 of Notes to Financial Statement for a description of the prior series of Preferred Stock.

Business Combination and Other Provisions

The Company's Restated Certificate of Incorporation requires that except in certain circumstances, Business Combinations between the Company and a beneficial holder of 10% or more of the Company's outstanding voting stock (an "Interested Stockholder") be approved by an affirmative vote of the holders of at least 67% of the voting power of the outstanding shares of the voting stock of the Company, voting together as a single class.

A Business Combination is defined generally in the Restated Certificate of Incorporation as (i) a merger or consolidation between or with the Company (which for these purposes includes subsidiaries of the Company) and an Interested Stockholder or a corporation which after the merger or consolidation would be an affiliate or associate of an Interested Stockholder, (ii) any sale, lease, exchange, mortgage, pledge, transfer or other disposition (in one transaction or a series of transactions) of more than 10% of the fair market value of the Company's assets to an Interested Stockholder or an affiliate or associate of an Interested Stockholder, (iii) the issuance, exchange or transfer by the Company to an Interested Stockholder or an affiliate or associate of an Interested Stockholder (in one transaction or a series of transactions) of any securities having a fair market value of more than 10% of the fair market value of the Company's assets; (iv) the adoption of any plan or proposal for the liquidation or dissolution of the Company proposed by or on behalf of an Interested Stockholder or an affiliate or an associate of an Interested Stockholder; (v) any reclassification of securities (including any reverse stock split) or reorganization that would directly or indirectly increase the proportionate share of the outstanding shares of any class of equity securities or securities of the Company convertible into such class of equity securities owned directly or indirectly by an Interested Stockholder, its affiliates or associates; or (vi) any agreement, contract or other arrangement with an Interested Stockholder (or in which the Interested Stockholder has an interest other than proportionately as a stockholder) providing for any one or more of the actions specified in (i) to (v).

The voting requirements outlined above will not apply, however, if the Business Combination was approved by a majority of the Board of Directors who at the time such approval was given were not affiliates or nominees of the Interested Stockholder and were members of the Board of Directors prior to the time the Interested Stockholder became an Interested Stockholder (the "Disinterested Directors") or are successors of Disinterested Directors who are not affiliates or nominees of the Interested Stockholder and who were recommended to succeed a Disinterested Director by a majority of the Disinterested Directors. Alternatively, such voting requirements will not apply if (a) the consideration to be received by the holders of each class of the Company's outstanding voting stock is at least equal to the greatest of (i) the highest per share price (including any brokerage commissions, transfer taxes and soliciting dealers' fees) paid by or on behalf of the Interested Stockholder for any shares of such class (A) within the two-year period immediately prior to the first public announcement of the proposal of the Business Combination, or (B) in a transaction in which it became an Interested Stockholder, (ii) the highest fair market value per share of such voting stock on (A) the date of the first public announcement of the Business Combination, or (B) the date on which the Interested Stockholder became an Interested Stockholder, (iii) the fair market value per share determined in accordance with the preceding clause (ii) multiplied by a fraction, the numerator of which is the highest price (including any brokerage commissions, transfer taxes and soliciting dealers' fees) paid for any share of such voting stock by the Interested Stockholder in the two-year period prior to announcement of the proposed Business Combination and the denominator of which is the fair market value per share of such voting stock on the first day in such two-year period in which the Interested Stockholder owned any shares of such voting stock, or (iv) (if applicable) the highest preferential amount per share to which the holders of shares of such class of voting stock (other than Common Stock) are entitled in the event of any liquidation, dissolution or winding up of the Company; (b) such consideration is in cash or in the same form of consideration as the Interested Stockholder paid to acquire the largest number of voting shares previously acquired by it; (c) except as approved by a majority of the Disinterested Directors, there shall have been no reduction in the annual rate of dividends paid on the Common Stock or a failure to declare and pay at the regular date therefor any full quarterly dividends on any outstanding preferred stock; (d) the Interested Stockholder must have refrained from acquiring additional shares of voting stock of the Corporation after it became an Interested Stockholder; (e) the Interested Stockholder has not received certain specified benefits from the Company, such as loans or guarantees; (f) a proxy or information statement complying with the Securities Exchange Act of 1934 must have been sent to the Company's stockholders at least 30 days prior to the proposed Business Combination; and (g) except with the approval of a majority of the Disinterested Directors, the Interested Stockholder must not have made any major change in the Company's business or equity capital structure. In the event that these requirements are satisfied, approval by holders of at least a majority of the outstanding voting stock of the Company will still be required under Delaware law to approve the Business Combination.

The Restated Certificate of Incorporation provides that any action required or permitted to be taken by the stockholders of the Company may be taken only at a duly called annual or special meeting of the stockholders or by unanimous written consent of the stockholders and may not be effected by a written consent not signed by all stockholders. Only a majority of the Board of Directors or the holders of at least 67% of the outstanding voting stock of the Company may call a special meeting of stockholders. These provisions, together with the provisions relating to Business Combinations summarized above, could have the effect of making it more difficult for a third party to acquire, or of discouraging a third party from acquiring, a majority of the outstanding voting stock of the Company, even if such a transaction would be beneficial to a majority of the Company's stockholders.

The Company recently adopted an amendment to its Restated Certificate of Incorporation, incorporating certain provisions permitted under recent revisions in Delaware law relating to the liability of directors. The amendment eliminates a director's liability for monetary damages for breach of fiduciary duty, including gross negligence, except in circumstances involving certain wrongful acts, such as the breach of a director's duty of loyalty or acts or omissions which involve intentional misconduct or a knowing violation of law. The new Delaware statute does not eliminate a director's duty of care and has no effect on the availability of equitable remedies such as injunction or rescission based upon a director's breach of the duty of care. In addition, the amendment does not apply to claims against a director for violation of certain laws, including Federal securities laws. The Company believes that the amendment will assist it in attracting and retaining qualified individuals to serve as directors.

Delaware law provides generally that the affirmative vote of a majority of the shares entitled to vote on the subject matter is required to amend a corporation's certificate of incorporation unless the certificate of incorporation requires a greater percentage. The Company's Restated Certificate of Incorporation requires the affirmative vote of the holders of at least 67% of the outstanding voting stock of the Company to amend or repeal any of the foregoing provisions.

Transfer Agent

The First National Bank of Boston is the transfer agent and registrar for the Company's Common Stock.

SHARES ELIGIBLE FOR FUTURE SALE

Upon completion of this offering, the Company will have outstanding 9,406,948 shares of Common Stock (assuming the United States Underwriters' over-allotment option is not exercised), based upon 7,656,948 shares outstanding at November 30, 1986. Of these shares, the 1,750,000 shares sold in this offering will be freely tradeable without restriction under the Securities Act of 1933, as amended (the "Act"), unless purchased by "affiliates" of the Company, as that term is defined in Rule 144 under the Act. All of the remaining shares (the "Restricted Shares") were issued and sold by the Company in private transactions in reliance upon the exemption contained in Section 4(2) of the Act or Regulation D promulgated thereunder. Of such shares, approximately 1,295,501 shares held for more than three years by stockholders who are not affiliates of the Company will be eligible for sale in the public market, in reliance on Rule 144(k) promulgated under the Act, on various dates during the 90-day period following the date of this Prospectus; however, approximately 837,715 of such shares are subject to stockholder agreements with the Underwriters which restrict the sale of such shares for 150 days from the date of this Prospectus (see "Underwriters") and an additional 128,500 of such shares are held by employees subject to restrictions on sale and a right of repurchase in favor of the Company in the event of termination of employment. Consequently, a total of 329,286 Restricted Shares will be eligible for sale in the public market without restriction during the 90-day period following the date of this Prospectus.

Approximately 5,051,120 Restricted Shares become eligible for sale under Rule 144 beginning 90 days after the date of this Prospectus. Sales of such shares are subject to volume limitations and other requirements applicable under Rule 144 as described below. However, approximately 4,631,493 of such shares are subject to stockholder agreements with the Underwriters which restrict the sale of such shares for 150 days from the date of this Prospectus (see "Underwriters"), and an additional 18,000 of such shares are held by employees subject to restrictions on sale and a right of repurchase in favor of the Company in the event of termination of employment. Consequently, a total of 401,627 additional Restricted Shares will be eligible for sale in the public market without restriction beginning 90 days after the date of this Prospectus.

The remaining approximately 1,310,327 Restricted Shares may not be sold pursuant to Rule 144 prior to the expiration of two years from the date of their respective purchases — that is, between May 17, 1987 and November 12, 1988.

In general, under Rule 144 as currently in effect, beginning 90 days after the date of this Prospectus an "affiliate" of the Company or person (or persons whose shares are aggregated) who has beneficially owned Restricted Shares for at least two years would be entitled to sell within any three-month period a number of shares that does not exceed the greater of 1% of the then outstanding shares of the Company's Common Stock (approximately 94,000 shares immediately after this offering assuming no exercise of the Underwriter's over-allotment option) or the average weekly trading volume in the over-the-counter market during the four calendar weeks preceding the date on which notice of the sale is filed with the Securities and Exchange Commission. Sales under Rule 144 are also subject to certain provisions relating to the manner of sale, notice requirements and availability of current public information about the Company. A person (or persons whose shares are aggregated) who is not deemed to have been an "affiliate" of the Company at any time during the 90 days preceding the sale and who has beneficially owned Restricted Shares for at least three years is entitled to sell such shares under Rule 144(k) without regard to the limitations described above.

Executive officers, directors and certain holders of more than 1% of the Company's shares (owning an aggregate of approximately 6,331,388 shares, or 67.3% of the outstanding shares of Common Stock immediately after this offering) have agreed not to offer, sell, contract to sell, grant any option to purchase or otherwise dispose of any shares of Common Stock for a period of 150 days after the date of this Prospectus, without the prior written consent of Morgan Stanley & Co. Incorporated and Hambrecht & Quist Incorporated. See "Underwriters."

Prior to this offering, there has been no market for the Common Stock of the Company and no prediction can be made as to the effect, if any, that market sales of shares or the availability of such shares for sale will have on the market price of the Common Stock prevailing from time to time. Nevertheless, sales of substantial amounts of Common Stock in the public market could adversely affect prevailing market prices and could impair the Company's future ability to raise capital through the sale of its equity securities.

The Company intends to file registration statements under the Act to register all shares of Common Stock reserved for issuance under the Restricted Plan and the Purchase Plan. These registration statements are expected to be filed approximately 90 days after the date of this Prospectus and are expected to become automatically effective 20 days after filing. Shares issued under the Restricted Plan and the Purchase Plan after the effective date of the registration statement generally will be available for sale to the public following the lapse of applicable vesting requirements.

The holders of shares of Common Stock of the Company issued upon conversion of the Preferred Stock and upon exercise of outstanding Warrants to acquire an aggregate of 19,107 shares of Common Stock (the "Registrable Shares"), are entitled to certain rights to register such shares for sale to the public under the Act. Under the terms of agreements between the Company and those holders, if the Company proposes to register any of its Common Stock for sale, those holders are entitled to include in that registration their Registrable Shares. subject to certain conditions and limitations. The holders of specified percentages of the Registrable Shares may require the Company, on not more than a total of two occasions, whether or not the Company proposes to register any of its Common Stock for sale, to register all or a part of their shares for sale to the public under the Act. In addition, holders of Registrable Shares may require the Company to register all or part of their shares on Form S-3 if the Company then qualifies for use of such form, subject to certain conditions and limitations. Generally, the Company is required to bear all of the expenses of such registrations. None of the shares of Common Stock offered hereby are being sold on behalf of any stockholders of the Company.

UNDERWRITERS

Under the terms and subject to the conditions contained in an Underwriting Agreement dated the date hereof, a syndicate of United States Underwriters (the "United States Underwriters") named below, including Morgan Stanley & Co. Incorporated and Hambrecht & Quist Incorporated, as representatives (the "Representatives"), and a syndicate of international underwriters (the "International Underwriters") named below, have severally agreed to purchase, and the Company has agreed to sell to them, the respective number of shares of the Company's Common Stock set forth opposite the name of such Underwriters below:

Name	Number of Shares
United States Underwriters	
Morgan Stanley & Co. Incorporated	298,525
Hambrecht & Quist Incorporated	298,525
Adams, Harkness & Hill, Inc.	6,650
Advest, Inc.	6,650
Allen & Company Incorporated	11,500
L. H. Alton & Company	3,600
Arnhold and S. Bleichroeder, Inc.	6,650
Robert W. Baird & Co. Incorporated	6,650
Bateman Eichler, Hill Richards Incorporated	6,650
Bear, Stearns & Co. Inc.	22,350
Sanford C. Bernstein & Co., Inc.	22,350
William Blair & Company	11,500
Blunt Ellis & Loewi Incorporated	6,650
J. C. Bradford & Co. Incorporated	6,650
Alex. Brown & Sons Incorporated	22,350
Boettcher & Company, Inc.	3,600
Cable, Howse & Ragen	11,500
Cowen & Co.	22,350
Dillon, Read & Co. Inc.	22,350
Doft & Co., Inc.	3,600
Donaldson, Lufkin & Jenrette Securities Corporation	22,350
Drexel Burnham Lambert Incorporated	22,350
Eberstadt Fleming Inc.	6,650
A. G. Edwards & Sons, Inc.	22,350
Fahnestock & Co. Inc.	3,600
First Albany Corporation	3,600
The First Boston Corporation	22,350
First Manhattan Co.	3,600
First of Michigan Corporation	6,650
Folger Nolan Fleming Douglas Inc.	3,600
Furman Selz Mager Dietz & Birney Incorporated	6,650
Gartner Securities Corporation	3,600
Goldman, Sachs & Co.	22,350
Hayes & Griffith, Inc.	3,600
E. F. Hutton & Company Inc.	22,350
Interstate Securities Corporation	6,650
Janney Montgomery Scott Inc.	6,650
Johnston, Lemon & Co. Incorporated	3,600
Kidder, Peabody & Co. Incorporated	22,350
Ladenburg, Thalmann & Co. Inc.	6,650
Laidlaw Adams & Peck Inc.	3,600
Cyrus J. Lawrence Incorporated	6,650
Lazard Freres & Co.	22,350
Legg Mason Wood Walker, Incorporated	6,650
McDonald & Company Securities, Inc.	11,500
Merrill Lynch, Pierce, Fenner & Smith Incorporated	22,350
Montgomery Securities	22,350
Moseley Securities Corporation	6,650
Needham & Company, Inc.	6,650

Name	Number of Shares
Neuberger & Berman	6,650
The Ohio Company	6,650
Oppenheimer & Co., Inc.	11,500
PaineWebber Incorporated	22,350
Parker/Hunter Incorporated	3,600
Piper, Jaffray & Hopwood Incorporated	11,500
Prescott, Ball & Turben, Inc.	11,500
Prudential-Bache Securities Inc.	22,350
Rauscher Pierce Refsnes, Inc.	6,650
Robertson, Colman & Stephens	22,350
Rotan Mosle Inc.	6,650
L. F. Rothschild, Unterberg, Towbin, Inc.	22,350
Salomon Brothers Inc	22,350
Shearson Lehman Brothers Inc.	22,350
Smith Barney, Harris Upham & Co. Incorporated	22,350
Stephens Inc.	6,650
Stifel, Nicolaus & Company Incorporated	6,650
Sutro & Co. Incorporated	6,650
Thomson McKinnon Securities Inc.	11,500
Tucker, Anthony & R. L. Day, Inc.	6,650
Volpe & Covington	3,600
Wertheim & Co., Inc.	22,350
Wheat, First Securities, Inc.	11,500
Dean Witter Reynolds Inc.	22,350
Subtotal	1,450,000

International Underwriters

Name	Number of Shares
Morgan Stanley International	80,000
Hambrecht & Quist Incorporated	80,000
Banque Indosuez	17,500
Cazenove & Co.	17,500
Goldman Sachs International Corp.	17,500
IMI Capital Markets (UK) Ltd.	17,500
Morgan Grenfell & Co. Limited	17,500
The Nikko Securities Co., (Europe) Ltd.	17,500
Salomon Brothers International Limited	17,500
Vereins- und Westbank Aktiengesellschaft	17,500
Subtotal	300,000
Total	1,750,000

The Underwriting Agreement provides that the obligations of the several Underwriters to pay for and accept delivery of the shares of Common Stock offered hereby are subject to the approval of certain legal matters by counsel and to certain other conditions, including the conditions that no stop order suspending the effectiveness of the Registration Statement is in effect and no proceedings for such purpose are pending before or threatened by the Securities and Exchange Commission, and that there has been no material adverse change in the business, financial condition or results of operations of the Company from that set forth in the Registration Statement. The Underwriters are obligated to take and pay for all of the shares of Common Stock offered hereby (other than those covered by the over-allotment option described below) if any such shares are taken.

Pursuant to the Underwriting Agreement, each United States Underwriter agrees that, as part of the distribution of the shares of Common Stock, (a) it is not purchasing any shares of Common Stock for the account of anyone other than a United States or Canadian Person and (b) it has not offered or sold, and will not offer or sell, directly or indirectly, any shares of Common Stock or distribute this Prospectus outside the United States or Canada or to anyone other than a United States or Canadian Person. Pursuant to the Underwriting Agreement, each International Underwriter agrees that, as part of the distribution of the shares of Common Stock, (a) it is not purchasing any shares of Common

Stock for the account of any United States or Canadian Person and (b) it has not offered or sold, and will not offer or sell, directly or indirectly, any shares of Common Stock or distribute this Prospectus within the United States or Canada or to any United States or Canadian Person. As used herein, "United States or Canadian Person" means any individual who is resident in the United States or Canada, or any corporation, pension, profit-sharing or other trust or other entity organized under or governed by the laws of the United States or Canada or any political subdivision thereof (other than a foreign branch of any United States or Canadian Person) and includes any United States or Canadian branch of anyone other than a United States or Canadian Person.

Pursuant to the Agreement between United States and International Underwriters, sales may be made between the United States Underwriters and the International Underwriters of any number of shares of Common Stock as may be mutually agreed. The per share price of any shares so sold shall be the initial public offering price less an amount not greater than the per share amount of "Underwriting Discounts and Commissions" set forth on the cover of this Prospectus.

Any offer of shares of Common Stock in Canada will be made only pursuant to an exemption from the requirement to file a prospectus in the relevant province of Canada in which such offer is made.

Offers of Common Stock may not be made in Great Britain except to persons whose ordinary business is to buy or sell shares or debentures, whether as principal or agent (except in circumstances which do not constitute an offer to the public within the meaning of the Companies Act 1985 of Great Britain), and unless the person making a distribution is a person permitted to do so under the securities laws of Great Britain, this document may not be distributed, in preliminary or final form, in or from Great Britain, other than to persons whose business involves the acquisition and disposal, or the holding, of securities, whether as principal or agent.

The Underwriters propose to offer part of the shares of Common Stock directly to the public at the public offering price set forth on the cover page hereof and part to dealers at a price which represents a concession not in excess of $.55 per share under the public offering price. The Underwriters may allow and such dealers may reallow a concession, not in excess of $.20 per share, to certain other dealers.

At the request of the Company, the Underwriters have reserved up to 140,000 of the shares of Common Stock offered hereby for sale at the public offering price to employees of the Company and certain persons with business and other relationships with the Company. Such persons must commit to purchase no later than the close of business on the day following the date hereof. The number of shares available for sale to the general public will be reduced to the extent such persons purchase such reserved shares. Any reserved shares not so purchased will be offered by the Underwriters to the general public on the same basis as the other shares offered hereby.

Pursuant to the Underwriting Agreement, the Company will grant to the United States Underwriters an option, exercisable for 30 days from the date of this Prospectus, to purchase up to 250,000 additional shares of Common Stock at the public offering price set forth on the cover page hereof less underwriting discounts and commissions. The United States Underwriters may exercise such option to purchase solely for the purpose of covering over-allotments, if any, incurred in connection with the sale of the shares of Common Stock offered hereby. To the extent such option is exercised, each United States Underwriter will become obligated, subject to certain conditions, to purchase approximately the same percentage of such additional shares as the number set forth next to such United States Underwriter's name in the preceding table bears to 1,450,000.

The Representatives have informed the Company that the Underwriters do not intend to confirm sales to any accounts over which they exercise discretionary authority.

The Company, executive officers, directors and certain holders of more than 1% of the Company's shares have agreed not to offer, sell, contract to sell, grant any option to purchase or otherwise dispose of any shares of Common Stock for a period of 150 days after the date of this Prospectus (subject, in the case of the Company, to certain limited exceptions) without the prior written consent of Morgan Stanley & Co. Incorporated and Hambrecht & Quist Incorporated, the Representatives of the Underwriters.

Venture capital funds affiliated with Morgan Stanley & Co. Incorporated, one of the Representatives of the Underwriters of this offering, purchased an aggregate of 37,037 shares of Series C Preferred Stock in March 1984 for a total purchase price of $249,999.75, and 65,000 shares of Series D Preferred Stock in December 1985 for a total purchase price of $650,000. All such shares will be converted into an aggregate of 102,037 shares of Common Stock upon the closing of this offering.

Thomas J. Perkins, a director of the Company, is Chairman of the Board of Directors of Morgan Stanley Ventures Inc., which is affiliated with Morgan Stanley & Co. Incorporated and is the general partner of Morgan Stanley Research Ventures L.P., a limited partnership that invests in research and development projects with technology companies. To date, Morgan Stanley Research Ventures L.P. has made no investment in the Company.

Venture capital funds managed by Hambrecht & Quist Venture Partners purchased an aggregate of 710,858 shares of Series B Preferred Stock in December 1982 for a total purchase price of $1,244,001.50, 444,444 shares of Series C Preferred Stock in March 1984 for a total purchase price of $2,999,997, and 550,000 shares of Series D Preferred Stock in December 1985 for a total purchase price of $5,500,000. All such shares will be converted into an aggregate of 1,705,302 shares of Common Stock upon the closing of this offering. Hambrecht & Quist Venture Partners is associated with Hambrecht & Quist Group, the parent company of Hambrecht & Quist Incorporated, one of the Representatives of the Underwriters of this offering.

Pricing of the Offering

Prior to this offering, there has been no public market for the Common Stock of the Company. Consequently, the initial public offering price for the Common Stock has been determined by negotiation between the Company and the Representatives of the Underwriters. Among the factors considered in determining the initial public offering price were the sales, earnings and certain other financial and operating information of the Company in recent periods, the future prospects of the Company and its industry in general and the price-earnings ratios, price-sales ratios, market prices of securities and certain financial and operating information of companies engaged in activities similar to those of the Company.

LEGAL OPINIONS

Certain legal matters with respect to the legality of the issuance of the Common Stock offered hereby are passed upon for the Company by Hale and Dorr, Boston, Massachusetts, and for the Underwriters by Davis Polk & Wardwell, New York, New York. Paul P. Brountas, a partner in the firm of Hale and Dorr, is Secretary of the Company. Certain partners of Hale and Dorr own an aggregate of 33,571 shares of Common Stock.

EXPERTS

The financial statements of the Company included in this Prospectus and the Registration Statement have been examined by Coopers & Lybrand, independent certified public accountants, as indicated in their reports with respect thereto. Such financial statements have been so included in reliance upon the authority of such firm as experts in auditing and accounting.

ADDITIONAL INFORMATION

A Registration Statement on Form S-1, including amendments thereto, relating to the Common Stock offered hereby has been filed by the Company with the Securities and Exchange Commission, Washington, D.C. This Prospectus does not contain all of the information set forth in the Registration Statement and the exhibits and schedules thereto. For further information with respect to the Company and the Common Stock offered hereby, reference is made to such Registration Statement, exhibits and schedules. Statements contained in this Prospectus as to the contents of any contract or other document referred to are not necessarily complete and in each instance reference is made to the copy of such contract or other document filed as an exhibit to the Registration Statement, each such statement being qualified in all respects by such reference. A copy of the Registration Statement may be inspected without charge at the Commission's principal offices in Washington, D.C. and copies of all or any part thereof may be obtained from the Commission upon the payment of certain fees prescribed by the Commission.

INDEX TO FINANCIAL STATEMENTS

REPORT OF INDEPENDENT CERTIFIED PUBLIC ACCOUNTANTS

To the Board of Directors and Stockholders of
Alliant Computer Systems Corporation:

We have examined the balance sheets of Alliant Computer Systems Corporation as of December 31, 1985 and 1984 and September 30, 1986 and the related statements of operations, stockholders' equity, and changes in financial position for each of the three years in the period ended December 31, 1985 and for the nine months ended September 30, 1986. Our examinations were made in accordance with generally accepted auditing standards and, accordingly, included such tests of the accounting records and such other auditing procedures as we considered necessary in the circumstances.

In our opinion, the financial statements referred to above present fairly the financial position of Alliant Computer Systems Corporation as of December 31, 1985 and 1984 and September 30, 1986, and the results of its operations and the changes in its financial position for each of the three years in the period ended December 31, 1985 and for the nine months ended September 30, 1986, in conformity with generally accepted accounting principles applied on a consistent basis.

COOPERS & LYBRAND

Boston, Massachusetts
November 3, 1986

ALLIANT COMPUTER SYSTEMS CORPORATION

BALANCE SHEETS

	December 31, 1984	December 31, 1985	September 30, 1986
ASSETS			
Current assets:			
Cash and cash equivalents (Note 1)	$ 8,292,640	$ 11,910,300	$ 5,099,811
Accounts receivable (Note 5)	—	2,282,466	8,313,102
Inventories (Notes 1, 2 and 5)	141,518	1,214,731	4,622,409
Prepaid expenses	14,873	26,157	146,153
Total current assets	8,449,031	15,433,654	18,181,475
Property and equipment net of accumulated depreciation and amortization (Notes 1, 3, 5 and 6)	786,757	1,336,437	5,047,597
Other assets	16,168	87,643	92,073
Total assets	$ 9,251,956	$ 16,857,734	$ 23,321,145
LIABILITIES AND STOCKHOLDERS' EQUITY			
Current liabilities:			
Notes payable — current portion (Note 6)	287,340	168,602	77,768
Accounts payable	291,455	446,691	3,083,034
Accrued expenses (Note 10)	132,934	953,008	2,159,096
Deferred service revenue (Note 1)	—	226,722	449,855
Total current liabilities	711,729	1,795,023	5,769,753
Notes payable, less current portion (Note 6)	270,688	61,100	—
Commitments (Note 9)			
Stockholders' equity (Note 7):			
Series A convertible preferred stock ($.01 par value); 500,000 shares authorized, issued and outstanding	5,000	5,000	5,000
Series B convertible preferred stock ($.01 par value); 2,742,857 shares authorized, issued and outstanding	27,429	27,429	27,429
Series C convertible preferred stock ($.01 par value); 1,480,526 shares authorized, issued and outstanding	14,805	14,805	14,805
Series D convertible preferred stock ($.01 par value); 1,500,000 shares authorized; 1,152,008 issued and outstanding at December 31, 1985 and September 30, 1986 (aggregate liquidation preference for all series preferred stock: $31,135,000 at September 30, 1986)	—	11,520	11,520
Common stock, $.01 par value; authorized 10,000,000 shares; issued and outstanding 1,635,238 shares at December 31, 1984, 1,662,210 shares at December 31, 1985, and 1,793,473 at September 30, 1986 (excluding 6,000 shares held in treasury at December 31, 1984 and 1985 and 11,000 shares held in treasury at September 30, 1986)	16,292	16,562	17,825
Additional paid-in capital	14,796,327	26,278,299	26,375,120
Accumulated deficit	(6,590,314)	(11,352,004)	(8,900,307)
Total stockholders' equity	8,269,539	15,001,611	17,551,392
Total liabilities and stockholders' equity	$ 9,251,956	$ 16,857,734	$ 23,321,145

The accompanying notes are an integral part of the financial statements.

ALLIANT COMPUTER SYSTEMS CORPORATION
STATEMENTS OF OPERATIONS

	For the Years Ended December 31,			For the Nine Months Ended September 30,	
	1983	1984	1985	1985	1986
				(unaudited)	
Net sales	—	—	$ 4,406,489	$ 293,002	$18,503,663
Cost of sales	—	—	2,415,788	272,553	6,858,181
Gross profit	—	—	1,990,701	20,449	11,645,482
Operating expenses:					
Research and development ..	$ 2,476,425	$ 3,897,927	4,450,342	3,621,048	3,521,417
Selling, general and administrative	269,091	817,111	2,611,018	1,717,946	5,998,024
Operating income (loss) ..	(2,745,516)	(4,715,038)	(5,070,659)	(5,318,545)	2,126,041
Interest income	306,156	851,493	354,896	335,034	502,322
Interest expense..............	(25,350)	(63,602)	(45,927)	(36,880)	(7,234)
Income (loss) before provision for income taxes and extraordinary credit.........	(2,464,710)	(3,927,147)	(4,761,690)	(5,020,391)	2,621,129
Provision for income taxes (Note 4)	—	—	—	—	1,313,285
Income (loss) before extraordinary credit.........	(2,464,710)	(3,927,147)	(4,761,690)	(5,020,391)	1,307,844
Extraordinary credit — tax benefit of loss carryforward..	—	—	—	—	1,143,853
Net income (loss)	$(2,464,710)	$(3,927,147)	$(4,761,690)	$(5,020,391)	$ 2,451,697
Income (loss) per share:					
Income (loss) before extraordinary credit.......	$(.39)	$(.50)	$(.58)	$(.61)	$.15
Extraordinary credit	—	—	—	—	.14
Net income (loss)	$(.39)	$(.50)	$(.58)	$(.61)	$.29
Weighted average number of common and common equivalent shares outstanding (Note 1)	6,354,933	7,909,057	8,169,121	8,166,169	8,431,294

The accompanying notes are an integral part of the financial statements.

ALLIANT COMPUTER SYSTEMS CORPORATION

STATEMENTS OF CHANGES IN STOCKHOLDERS' EQUITY
for the years ended December 31, 1985, 1984 and 1983
and the nine months ended September 30, 1986

	Preferred Stock		Common Stock		Additional Paid-in Capital	Accumulated Deficit	Total Stockholders' Equity
	Number of Shares	Par Value	Number of Shares	Par Value			
Balance at January 1, 1983	3,242,857	$32,429	1,050,000	$10,500	$ 4,887,571	$ (198,457)	$ 4,732,043
Sale of common stock			549,500	5,495	21,980		27,475
Net loss						(2,464,710)	(2,464,710)
Balance at December 31, 1983	3,242,857	32,429	1,599,500	15,995	4,909,551	(2,663,167)	2,294,808
Sale of common stock			27,000	270	1,080		1,350
Sale of Series C preferred stock	1,480,526	14,805			9,850,031		9,864,836
Issuance of common stock			8,738	87	35,905		35,992
Repurchase of 6,000 shares of common stock				(60)	(240)		(300)
Net loss						(3,927,147)	(3,927,147)
Balance at December 31, 1984	4,723,383	47,234	1,635,238	16,292	14,796,327	(6,590,314)	8,269,539
Exercise of stock options			19,000	190	13,110		13,300
Issuance of common stock			7,972	80	6,302		6,382
Sale of Series D preferred stock	1,152,008	11,520			11,462,560		11,474,080
Net loss						(4,761,690)	(4,761,690)
Balance at December 31, 1985	5,875,391	58,754	1,662,210	16,562	26,278,299	(11,352,004)	15,001,611
Issuance of common stock			13,500	135	13,365		13,500
Exercise of stock options			117,763	1,178	83,656		84,834
Repurchase of 5,000 shares of common stock				(50)	(200)		(250)
Net income						2,451,697	2,451,697
Balance at September 30, 1986	5,875,391	$58,754	1,793,473	$17,825	$26,375,120	$ (8,900,307)	$17,551,392

The accompanying notes are an integral part of the financial statements.

ALLIANT COMPUTER SYSTEMS CORPORATION

STATEMENTS OF CHANGES IN FINANCIAL POSITION

	For the Years Ended December 31,			For the Nine Months Ended September 30,	
	1983	1984	1985	1985 (unaudited)	1986
Funds (used in) provided by operations:					
Net income (loss) before extraordinary credit	$(2,464,710)	$(3,927,147)	$(4,761,690)	$(5,020,391)	$ 1,307,844
Items not requiring funds:					
Issuance of common stock	—	35,990	3,710	3,710	13,500
Depreciation and amortization	202,247	394,890	553,780	405,482	792,731
	(2,262,463)	(3,496,267)	(4,204,200)	(4,611,199)	2,114,075
Decrease (increase) in:					
Accounts receivable	—	—	(2,282,466)	(188,242)	(6,030,636)
Inventory	—	(141,518)	(1,073,213)	(2,038,990)	(3,407,678)
Prepaid expenses	(7,935)	2,213	(11,284)	(13,517)	(119,996)
Accounts payable	223,309	20,059	155,236	489,345	2,636,343
Accrued expenses	60,724	50,119	820,074	503,123	1,206,088
Deferred revenue	—	—	226,722	182,040	223,133
Funds used in operations	(1,986,365)	(3,565,394)	(6,369,131)	(5,677,440)	(3,378,671)
Extraordinary credit	—	—	—	—	1,143,853
Additions to property and equipment, net	(999,193)	(364,090)	(1,103,460)	(380,781)	(4,503,891)
Decrease (increase) in other assets	5,085	(33)	(71,475)	(11,080)	(4,430)
Funds provided (used) by financing sources:					
Sale of preferred stock	—	9,864,836	11,474,080	—	—
Sale of common stock	27,475	1,350	2,672	—	—
Purchase of treasury stock	—	(300)	—	—	(250)
Exercise of stock options	—	—	13,300	2,800	84,834
Proceeds from notes payable	662,000	200,000	650,000	—	—
Repayment of notes payable	(77,748)	(226,224)	(978,326)	(255,691)	(151,934)
Total funds provided (used) by financing sources	611,727	9,839,662	11,161,726	(252,891)	(67,350)
Net increase (decrease) in cash and cash equivalents	(2,368,746)	5,910,145	3,617,660	(6,322,192)	(6,810,489)
Cash and cash equivalents, beginning of period	4,751,241	2,382,495	8,292,640	8,292,640	11,910,300
Cash and cash equivalents, end of period	$ 2,382,495	$ 8,292,640	$11,910,300	$ 1,970,448	$ 5,099,811

The accompanying notes are an integral part of the financial statements.

ALLIANT COMPUTER SYSTEMS CORPORATION
NOTES TO FINANCIAL STATEMENTS

1. Summary of Significant Accounting Policies:

Nature of Business

Alliant Computer Systems Corporation, the "Company", operates in one industry segment and was formed to design, manufacture and market high-performance computer systems. Prior to September 1985, the Company was a development stage enterprise as its activities were primarily directed toward organizing the Company, recruiting employees and developing products. Commercial shipments of the Company's FX/series of computer systems began in September of 1985.

Interim Financial Information

The financial statements for the nine months ended September 30, 1985 are unaudited but include all adjustments (consisting only of normal recurring adjustments) which are, in the opinion of management, necessary for a fair statement of the results for the interim period. The interim results for the nine months ended September 30, 1986 are not necessarily indicative of results to be expected for the year ending December 31, 1986.

Cash and Cash Equivalents

Cash equivalents, which consist primarily of short-term commercial paper are carried at cost plus accrued interest, which approximates market.

Inventory

Inventory is stated at the lower of cost, determined under the first-in, first-out (FIFO) method, or market.

Property and Equipment

Property and equipment are stated at cost. Depreciation is computed using the straight-line method over estimated useful lives of the assets as follows:

Computer equipment	3 years
Office equipment	5 years
Leasehold improvements	Life of related lease

Maintenance, repairs and renewals are charged to expense as incurred. Additions and significant improvements are capitalized and depreciated. Upon retirement or sale, the cost of the assets disposed of and the related accumulated depreciation are removed from the accounts and any resulting gain or loss is included in the determination of net income.

Revenue Recognition

Revenue from equipment sales is recognized upon shipment. Revenue from service agreements is recognized ratably over the term of the agreement. Revenues in the fourth quarter of 1985 included approximately $1,687,000 of computer systems shipped in earlier periods. These systems were shipped to test sites for customer evaluation and were subsequently purchased.

Research and Development

Research and product development costs are expensed as incurred. During 1986, the Company adopted Statement of Financial Accounting Standard No. 86, "Accounting for the Costs of Computer

ALLIANT COMPUTER SYSTEMS CORPORATION
NOTES TO FINANCIAL STATEMENTS — (Continued)

Software to be Sold, Leased, or Otherwise Marketed." However, no costs of internally developed software were capitalized as the amounts qualifying for capitalization were immaterial.

Tax Credits

Investment tax credits and research and experimentation tax credits are accounted for as a reduction of the provision for income taxes in the year utilized, in accordance with the flow-through method.

Warranty

The Company provides a warranty for parts and labor on its products, generally for 90 days from the date of installation. The estimated cost of providing such warranty service on products sold is included in cost of sales at the time the associated revenue is recognized.

Net Income (Loss) per Common Share

Income per common and common equivalent share is computed using the weighted average number of common and dilutive common equivalent shares outstanding during the period. Dilutive common equivalent shares consist of stock options and warrants (using the treasury stock method). Pursuant to Securities and Exchange Commission Staff Accounting Bulletin (SAB) No. 55, common shares issued by the Company during the twelve months immediately preceding the offering date plus the number of common equivalent shares which were issued during the same period pursuant to the grant of stock options and warrants (using the treasury stock method and the proposed public offering price) have been included in the calculation of common and common equivalent shares as if they were outstanding for all periods presented. In addition, pursuant to the policy of the Staff of the Securities and Exchange Commission, the calculation also includes preferred stock as if converted to common stock on their respective original dates of issuance.

2. Inventory:

Inventory consists of the following:

	December 31,		September 30,
	1984	1985	1986
Raw materials	$141,518	$ 701,131	$2,783,227
Work in process	—	267,275	1,326,598
Finished goods	—	246,325	512,584
	$141,518	$1,214,731	$4,622,409

3. Property and Equipment:

Property and equipment consist of the following:

	December 31,		September 30,
	1984	1985	1986
Computer equipment	$1,290,017	$2,154,047	$6,442,754
Office equipment	10,685	14,712	24,256
Leasehold improvements	82,676	102,352	277,730
	1,383,378	2,271,111	6,744,740
Less accumulated depreciation and amortization..	(596,621)	(934,674)	(1,697,143)
	$ 786,757	$1,336,437	$5,047,597

4. Income Taxes:

For the nine months ended September 30, 1986, the Company has provided for income taxes at an effective rate of approximately 50.1%, consisting of Federal income taxes at the statutory rate of 46% and state income taxes, net of Federal income tax benefit, of approximately 4.1%. Income taxes have

ALLIANT COMPUTER SYSTEMS CORPORATION
NOTES TO FINANCIAL STATEMENTS — (Continued)

not been provided for any periods through December 31, 1985, as the Company incurred net operating losses in those periods.

For the nine months ended September 30, 1986, the Company recognized a tax benefit of $1,143,853 related to the utilization of net operating loss carryforwards. Such tax benefit has been reported as an extraordinary credit in the Statement of Operations.

At December 31, 1985 the Company had net operating loss carryforwards of approximately $11,352,000 for financial reporting purposes and approximately $11,458,000 for tax reporting purposes. The difference between the net operating loss carryforwards for tax and financial reporting results from timing differences in the recognition of certain expenses, principally depreciation and inventory-related items. For tax purposes, these carryforwards are available to reduce future federal taxable income during years extending through 1997 and 2000. For financial reporting purposes, the tax benefit, if any, from the utilization of these carryforwards will be recognized as an extraordinary credit in the year of utilization.

At December 31, 1985 the Company had, for both financial and tax reporting purposes, federal investment tax credit carryforwards of approximately $89,000 and research and experimentation credit carryforwards of approximately $880,000 that are available to offset future federal income taxes in years extending through 1997 and 2000. The Tax Reform Act of 1986 is not expected to have a material impact on the Company's annual results for 1986.

5. Line of Credit:

During 1985 the Company entered into a revolving line of credit agreement with a commercial bank. The agreement permits borrowings up to $4,000,000 (limited by the levels of certain accounts receivable and inventory as defined in the agreement), with interest at the bank's prime rate plus ½%. The Company agreed to maintain compensating balances with the lender equal to 5% of the commitment and 5% of the borrowings outstanding. In October 1986, the Company increased its borrowing limit to $10,000,000, with interest at the bank's prime rate plus ¼%. The Company has agreed to maintain compensating balances equal to 3.8% of the commitment, 2.5% of the first $5,000,000 of outstanding borrowings and 5% of outstanding borrowings over $5,000,000. Substantially all of the Company's assets serve as collateral under the line. At December 31, 1985 and September 30, 1986 there were no outstanding borrowings under the agreement.

6. Notes Payable:

Notes payable consist of installment notes payable under an equipment financing agreement. Under the terms of the agreement, the Company may borrow up to $950,000, with interest at the bank's prime rate plus ½%. At September 30, 1986 borrowings of $77,768 were outstanding and are collateralized by equipment with a net book value of approximately $34,500. Principal payments on such borrowings are due in 1987.

The weighted average annual interest rate on these notes payable for the years ended December 31, 1985, 1984, 1983 and for the nine months ended September 30, 1986 was 12.0%, 13.0%, 11.8% and 8.8%, respectively.

7. Capital Stock:

Convertible Preferred Stock

During 1985, the Company's stockholders adopted an amendment to the Company's Certificate of Incorporation increasing the number of authorized shares of preferred stock from 5,000,000 shares to 7,500,000 shares.

ALLIANT COMPUTER SYSTEMS CORPORATION

NOTES TO FINANCIAL STATEMENTS — (Continued)

Each share of Series A, B, C and D preferred stock is convertible into common stock on a one-for-one basis, except that the conversion rate will be adjusted for certain issuances of common stock which are dilutive in nature. The holders of preferred stock are entitled to receive non-cumulative dividends out of legally available assets prior and in preference to payment of dividends to common stockholders. The holders of Series A preferred stock are entitled to an amount per share at least equal to the amount of any common stock dividend. The holders of shares of Series B, C and D preferred stock are entitled to the greater of dividends at the rate of $.1575, $.6075 and $.90, respectively, per share per annum or the amount per share to be paid to Series A preferred stockholders. The holders of preferred stock are entitled to one vote for each share of common stock into which their stock is convertible. Series A, Series B, Series C and Series D stockholders are entitled to vote as separate classes on certain matters.

In the event of liquidation, and before any distribution to common stockholders, each preferred stockholder is entitled to receive an amount per share equal to the original issue price ($.22 for Series A, $1.75 for Series B, $6.75 for Series C and $10.00 for Series D) plus any declared and unpaid dividends. Additionally, Series B, C and D preferred stockholders are entitled to receive 9% per annum on the original issue price from the date of issuance to the date of liquidation, but not to exceed two times the original issue price. At September 30, 1986 the aggregate liquidation preference approximated $31,135,000.

Upon the closing of the Company's initial public offering, each outstanding share of Series A, Series B, Series C and Series D preferred stock will be automatically converted into one share of common stock. The preferred stock so converted will be canceled and may not thereafter be reissued. Effective upon the filing of a Restated Certificate of Incorporation, to be filed immediately following the consummation of the sale of common stock in its initial public offering, the Company will have a new authorized class of Series preferred stock consisting of 7,500,000 shares. Such Series preferred stock may be issued in series with such rights, preferences and privileges as the Board of Directors may determine.

Common Stock

Common stock has full voting rights. Dividend and liquidation rights are subject to those of the preferred stock. Effective upon the filing of an amendment to the Restated Certificate of Incorporation prior to the consummation of the sale of common stock in its initial public offering, the authorized common shares will be increased from 10,000,000 shares to 25,000,000 shares.

At September 30, 1986, 5,875,391 shares of common stock are reserved for conversion of the Company's Series A, B, C and D convertible preferred stock, 19,107 shares are reserved for exercise of warrants and 922,486 shares are reserved for exercise of employee stock options.

Restricted Stock and Stock Option Plan

In 1984 the Company adopted a Restricted Stock and Stock Option Plan (the "Plan") for its employees and consultants. The Plan, which is administered by the Board of Directors, permits the Company to sell restricted stock or grant stock options for the purchase of the Company's common stock, up to a maximum of 1,300,000 shares.

The Plan provides for the granting of Incentive Stock Options (ISOs) and Non-Statutory Options. In the case of ISOs the exercise price shall be not less than 100% (110% in certain cases) of the fair market value of the common stock as determined by the Board of Directors on the date of grant. In the case of Non-Statutory Options the exercise price shall be not less than 90% of the fair market value of the common stock as determined by the Board of Directors on the date of the grant. The options

ALLIANT COMPUTER SYSTEMS CORPORATION
NOTES TO FINANCIAL STATEMENTS — (Continued)

become exercisable generally six months from date of grant and expire ten years (five years for ISOs in certain cases) after the date of grant. The Company has the right to repurchase shares issued under the Plan upon termination of employment at the same price as paid by the employee. This repurchase right lapses as to 20% of the option shares each year from the date of grant.

Stock option activity under the Plan through the nine months ended September 30, 1986 was as follows:

	Number of Shares	Option Price Per Share
Options granted in 1984	133,750	$ .70
Outstanding at December 31, 1984	133,750	.70
Granted	287,205	.70 – 1.00
Exercised	19,000	.70
Outstanding at December 31, 1985	401,955	.70 – 1.00
Granted	660,010	1.00 – 2.00
Exercised	117,763	.70 – 1.00
Canceled	21,716	.70 – 1.25
Outstanding at September 30, 1986	922,486	$ .70 – 2.00

At September 30, 1986, 525,426 options are exercisable at prices of $.70–$2.00 and 221.951 shares are reserved for future sales of restricted stock or future grants of stock options. During the year ended December 31, 1985 and the nine months ended September 30, 1986, the Company issued 5,300 shares and 13,500 shares of restricted stock, respectively, under the Plan.

Employee Stock Purchase Plan

In 1986 the Company adopted an Employee Stock Purchase Plan (the "Purchase Plan"). Under the Purchase Plan employees may be granted rights, in semi-annual offering periods, to purchase common stock at the lower of 85% of the fair market value of the stock at the commencement of the offering period or at the end of the offering period. Common stock reserved for issuance under the Purchase Plan aggregated 300,000 shares at September 30, 1986. There were no rights granted under the Purchase Plan for the nine months ended September 30, 1986.

Stock Warrants

The Company granted warrants in connection with exclusive marketing and product development agreements for the purchase of 19,107 shares of common stock. The warrants are exercisable at prices of $.70 and $1.75 per share. The Company has the right to repurchase the warrants and such rights lapse in cumulative monthly installments over a 65-month period commencing on the date of issue. At September 30, 1986, 14,704 warrants were exercisable.

8. Major Customer:

During the year ended December 31, 1985, the Company had sales in excess of 10% of net sales to three customers constituting 59%, 25%, and 12%, respectively. During the nine months ended September 30, 1986, the Company had sales in excess of 10% of net sales to two customers constituting 21% and 12%, respectively.

ALLIANT COMPUTER SYSTEMS CORPORATION
NOTES TO FINANCIAL STATEMENTS — (Continued)

9. Commitments:

Operating Leases

The Company leases its manufacturing and office facilities under operating leases. In August 1986 the Company occupied a new facility which serves as its corporate headquarters and principal manufacturing facility. The lease for this facility has an initial term of five years with the option to extend for two additional five-year periods. The lease agreement requires the Company to pay all property taxes, insurance and maintenance costs.

Aggregate future minimum rental payments under all operating leases are as follows:

1986	$ 721,000
1987	1,158,000
1988	1,149,000
1989	1,114,000
1990	1,072,000
Thereafter	716,000
	$5,930,000

Rent expense charged to operations amounted to $229,000, $142,000, $101,000, $528,000 and $160,000 (unaudited) for the years ended December 31, 1985, 1984, and 1983 and the nine months ended September 30, 1986, and September 30, 1985, respectively.

Other

During 1986 the Company entered into marketing agreements with third-party software companies under which the Company is committed to future minimum royalty payments of approximately $300,000. These commitments will become payable at various times through March 1991.

10. Accrued Expenses:

Accrued expenses consist of the following:

	December 31, 1984	December 31, 1985	September 30, 1986
Accrued payroll and payroll related expenses	$ 7,331	$180,325	$ 499,577
Accrued commissions	—	124,000	389,545
Accrued warranty	—	163,800	186,409
Accrued other	125,603	484,883	1,083,565
	$132,934	$953,008	$2,159,096

Glossary

Glossary

agreement among underwriters—An agreement signed by the members of an underwriting syndicate (usually independent investment banking firms) that has been formed for a specific securities offering. The agreement authorizes the managing underwriter to sign a purchase agreement with the company that is selling the stock and to perform certain other functions on behalf of the syndicate.

all hands meeting—A meeting of all the parties involved in the preparation of the registration statement, including the company's owners and management, the company's legal counsel, the company's independent public accountants, the underwriter, and the underwriter's legal counsel. The first all hands meeting usually establishes the timetable for the offering and each participant's tasks, duties, and responsibilities related to the preparation of the registration statement and related documents.

all-or-none underwriting—A type of best efforts underwriting with the proviso that if the underwriters are unsuccessful in selling all the shares, then none of the shares is considered sold. The underwriter is under no contractual obligation to purchase any unsold shares. During the offering, the securities and the proceeds are held in a form of escrow arrangement pending the outcome of the offering. The money is returned to the investors if all the shares are not sold in the offering.

analyst—An individual, employed by an investment banking firm or other financial institution, who studies and analyzes the operations, financial performance, and condition of individual companies or industries for the purpose of providing investment advice.

bailout—An offering which, for a variety of reasons, gives the appearance that the selling stockholders are selling their stock or reducing their ownership in the company because they have lost confidence or interest in the future of the company. The usual characteristic of a bailout is an offering in which an excessive portion of the shares being sold is for the account of the selling shareholders, and is not new shares being offered by the company to raise additional capital.

best efforts underwriting—A type of underwriting agreement in which the underwriters, acting as agents for the issuer, agree only to use their best efforts to sell the shares being offered and are not committed to purchase any unsold shares.

bid and asked—The prices quoted for trading in the over-the-counter market. The "Bid" is the highest price someone is willing to pay; the "Asked" is the lowest price at which someone is willing to sell. The difference between the two is referred to as the "spread."

"blue sky" laws—The name used to refer to the various states' securities laws created to protect their citizens against securities fraud. The laws vary from state to state.

"blue sky" memorandum—A summary, usually prepared by the underwriters' legal counsel, indicating the states in which the offering may be made, and the conditions, restrictions, and provisions applicable to offering the securities in each of those states.

book value per share—Derived directly from the balance sheet of the company, it is the equity value of an outstanding share of stock and is computed by dividing the net worth of the company (assets minus liabilities) by the number of shares outstanding.

broker/dealer—A broker is an agent who acts as a middleman to buy or sell securities on behalf of his clients. A dealer buys stocks for his own account and sells to a customer from his inventory of stocks.

capitalization—The company's long-term debt and equity structure.

cheap (promotional) stock—Stock or instruments convertible to stock (warrants, options, rights, etc.) issued to certain individuals within a certain period prior to a public offering which might yield an unreasonable amount of profit to the holders and be deemed unfair and inequitable to the public investors.

closing—The final meeting, at which the company delivers the securities sold and receives the proceeds of the offering.

"cold comfort" letter—A colloquial name given to the letter written by the company's independent accountants to the underwriter indicating the tests and procedures performed on the company's financial data and the results of such work. The underwriter requests such tests as part of his due diligence review.

control (controlling, controlled by, under the control of)—A person's direct or indirect possession of the power (whether through ownership of voting shares, by contract, or otherwise) to direct, or cause the direction of, a company's management policies.

deficiency (comment) letter—A letter from the SEC with comments on any deficiencies noted in its review of the registration statement.

dilution—The reduction in one's equity interest caused by the difference between a public offering price per share that is higher than the pre-offering tangible book value per share.

directors' and officers' questionnaires—A series of questions and disclosure requests circulated by the company's counsel and the underwriters' counsel with the purpose of soliciting and verifying the information that will be disclosed in the registration statement.

"dog and pony show"—A colloquial name given to the series of presentations made to potential investors, analysts, and underwriters by the company's management during the waiting period. Sometimes referred to as the *road show*.

due diligence—The requirement that those persons responsible for preparing and signing the registration statement have performed a reasonable investigation to form a basis for believing that the statements and information contained in the registration statement are true, and that no material facts have been omitted.

effective date—The date on which the registration statement becomes effective and the sale of the securities can commence.

financial printer—A printer who has the special expertise required to layout, typeset, and print financial documents such as the registration statement and prospectus.

firm commitment underwriting—A type of underwriting agreement in which the underwriters commit to buy all the shares in the offering at an agreed upon price and take the risk of reselling them to the public and institutional investors at the offering price. If all the shares are not sold, the underwriters will hold the unsold shares for their own account.

float—The hypothetical number of shares considered available for trading in the public market. The float is calculated by deducting the number of shares held by insiders or institutional investors from the total shares outstanding. A small float may preclude interest by institutional investors who are concerned with the liquidity of their investment and abnormal price movements due to the law of supply and demand.

Foreign Corrupt Practices Act—A federal law that requires public companies to maintain adequate records and systems of internal control.

Form 8-K—A report required to be filed with the SEC by a public company when certain material events occur.

Form 10-K—The special annual report that a public company must file with the SEC.

Form 10-Q—The special quarterly report that a public company must file with the SEC.

Form S-1—The registration statement with the most extensive and comprehensive information requirements, used by companies that are not eligible to use any of the other, less extensive registration statements.

Form S-18—A registration statement with less extensive technical and financial disclosure requirements, but limited to a maximum offering of $7.5 million.

Form S-R—A report periodically filed with the SEC after an initial public offering, describing how the proceeds of the offering were used.

"green shoe"—The colloquial name for an option given to the underwriters allowing the underwriters to purchase additional shares of stock from the company (and/or the selling shareholders) to cover over-allotments. The option is usually equal to a maximum of 10 percent of the number of shares in the offering.

initial public offering (IPO)—The first-time offering of a company's stock to the public.

insider trading—The purchase or sale of the company's stock by officers, directors, and certain others with access to nonpublic information concerning the company. Specific rules must be adhered to when an insider wishes to buy or sell a public company's stock.

institutional investor—a generic name for an organization with a large accumulation of capital for investment in the securities market, such as an insurance company, pension fund, trust or mutual fund.

investment banker—An individual or organization that provides advice and services relating to raising capital, financing, mergers, acquisitions, and certain other business activities. An investment banker can also function as an underwriter.

letter of intent—A non-binding, preliminary agreement between the underwriters and the company confirming the underwriters' intent to proceed with the offering and specifying the general terms to be included in the final underwriting agreement.

making a market—The activities of the managing underwriter and his syndicate after the initial offering, when they buy and sell shares of the company's stock on the open market, provide research analyst coverage, and sponsor programs to develop and maintain investor interest.

managing underwriter—The firm with whom the company deals in the preparation of the registration statement and negotiation of all matters related to the offering; the lead underwriter of an underwriting syndicate.

market-maker—The term used for a dealer when he maintains trading activity in a particular security by openly offering to buy or sell that security at firm bid and asked prices.

material—When referring to required financial information, material information is anything about which the average prudent investor ought reasonably to be informed. There are no hard and fast rules to govern this determination except integrity, common sense, and the realities and dangers of hindsight judgment in the event of the omission of material information.

minimum percentage underwriting—A type of best efforts underwriting with the proviso that if a certain pre-set minimum percentage of the offering is sold, then the offering is considered accomplished regardless of any remaining balance of unsold shares.

National Association of Securities Dealers (NASD)—An association of broker-dealers in the over-the-counter market. In addition to having a series of standards and guidelines for professional conduct, the association reviews underwriters' compensation arrangements in public offerings to determine if they are fair and reasonable.

National Association of Securities Dealers Automated Quotations (NASDAQ)—A communications network among broker-dealers which provides bid and asked price information as well as trading volume on stocks traded in the over-the-counter market. A company's stock is identified by a symbol, usually composed of letters taken from the company's name.

over-allotment—An underwriter's offer to sell more shares in an offering than it has agreed to purchase from the issuing company.

over-the-counter (OTC) market—A market conducted by securities dealers not listed on a stock exchange. Prices on this market are arrived at by negotiation. On an exchange, prices are arrived at by a two-way auction process.

person—Used in connection with SEC matters, a person is an individual, a corporation, a partnership, an association, a joint-stock company, a business trust, or an unincorporated organization.

"pink sheets"—A colloquial name for the daily list of bid and asked prices over-the-counter stocks not trading on the NASDAQ system.

price/earnings (P/E) ratio—A measurement of stock value computed by dividing the price per share of a common stock by the earnings per share.

pricing amendment—The final amendment to the registration statement, disclosing the final price of the offering.

primary offering—An offering consisting entirely of previously unissued shares. The proceeds of such an offering go to the issuing company.

private placement—The sale of securities through a non-public offering that is exempt from registration under certain restrictions and conditions.

prospectus—The selling document for an offering. It is included as Part I of the registration statement and discloses pertinent information concerning the company and the offering. It is also distributed to potential and actual buyers of the stock at the offering.

"quiet period"—The colloquial name for the time period between the signing of a letter of intent and 90 days after the actual offering starts. During this period, the form and nature of publicity concerning the company are severely restricted.

"red herring"—The colloquial name for the preliminary prospectus circulated to prospective buyers by the underwriting syndicate while waiting for the registration statement to be declared effective by the SEC. A legend in red ink appears on the cover stating that the registration statement has not yet become effective.

registrar—An agency that performs services relating to the issuance of share certificates to new shareholders and makes certain that the number of new shares issued is the same as the number of shares cancelled as the result of sales, exchanges, and other transfers.

registration statement—The document filed with the SEC to register securities in conformity with federal law. The registration statement is a disclosure document and consists of the prospectus (Part I) and supplemental information and exhibits (Part II).

Regulation A—An SEC regulation governing public offerings of less than $1.5 million which are exempt from registration. Transactions exempt from registration are not exempt from federal antifraud statutes.

Regulation D—An SEC regulation governing private placement offerings which are exempt from registration. Transactions exempt from registration are not exempt from federal antifraud statutes.

Regulation S-K—An SEC regulation governing the non-financial-statement disclosures in the registration statements and other documents filed with the SEC.

Regulation S-X—An SEC regulation governing the preparation of financial statement disclosures in the registration statements and other documents filed with the SEC.

reporting person—An officer or director of a public company, or any beneficial holder of more than 10 percent of any class of stock in the company, who must file certain reports with the SEC regarding his stock ownership and any changes thereto.

restricted stock—Shares of stock with limitations on their resale or transferability, sometimes referred to as *lettered stock*. A legend is often placed on the share certificates indicating such restrictions.

Rule 144—The rule that allows, under certain conditions, the non-registered public sale of restricted stock and stock owned by controlling stockholders.

secondary offering—An offering in which all the securities being offered were previously unregistered and owned by existing stockholders. The proceeds of such an offering go to the selling shareholders. A **partial secondary offering** is one in which the securities being offered are from existing stockholders and from the company. The proceeds of such an offering are usually divided proportionately between the company and the selling stockholders.

Securities Act of 1933—The statutes dealing with the disclosure requirements for securities offered and sold in interstate commerce.

Securities and Exchange Commission (SEC)—The federal agency established by Congress to administer federal securities laws.

Securities Exchange Act of 1934—The statutes that regulate the securities markets and exchanges, and related procedures, reports, and practices.

short sale—The practice in which shares are sold first and bought later, in expectation that the market price of that stock will go down, thereby permitting a profit to be made when the short position is "covered" by the later purchase.

"short-swing" profits—Profits made by reporting persons as the result of the purchase-then-sale or sale-then-purchase of any security of the company within a six-month period. Such profits are prohibited and are subject to recapture by the company.

stabilization—The underwriters' purchase of shares for their own account in an attempt to stabilize the price of a new issue that has dropped below its original offering price.

syndicate—Two or more investment bankers who form a temporary arrangement to underwrite and/or market a specific offering.

"tombstone" ad—The colloquial name for a stylized advertisement announcing the offering and the name(s) of the underwriter(s).

transfer agent—An agency which performs services for the company by keeping the official records of the names, addresses, and shareholdings of the stockholders and handling the transfer of shares.

treasury stock—Stock issued by a company then reacquired by the company. These shares may be reissued, retired, or held in the company's treasury. Treasury stock has no voting rights and does not receive dividends.

underwriter—An organization which, under certain terms and conditions, is compensated to serve as the middleman in offering a company's shares to the public. Two or more underwriters can join together to form an underwriting syndicate.

underwriting agreement—The contract between a company and its underwriter(s) which sets forth the terms of the offering, including the type of underwriting, the underwriters' compensation, the offering price, the number of shares to be offered and certain other matters. This contract is usually not signed until 24 hours prior to the anticipated effect date of the registration statement.

waiting period—The period of time between the date the registration statement is first filed with the SEC and the date the registration statement is declared effective.

warrant—A certificate that gives the holder the right to purchase securities at a stipulated price within a specified time (or sometimes perpetually). Warrants can have significant market value based upon the differential between the purchase price permitted in the warrant and the current market value of the securities.

Index

Index